Subtle Serpent

New Age
in the
Classroom

Subtle Serpent

New Age in the Classroom

**DARYLANN WHITEMARSH
AND BILL REISMAN**

HUNTINGTON HOUSE PUBLISHERS

Huntington House Publishers
P.O. Box 53788
Lafayette, Louisiana 70505

Library of Congress Card Catalog Number
92-73281
ISBN 1-56384-016-2

Dedication

To those who love children; those who are called upon to be social worker, minister, babysitter, parent, counselor, role model, confidant, authority figure, friend, guide, and disciplinarian; to those we pay so little for so important a job. When the rest of the world is negative and skeptical about the future of our young people, these people show up, prepared, day in and day out, refusing to give in. They see the positive. They stake claim on the future by preparing young minds to be practically prepared and to dream dreams.

To the teachers of America, we say thanks!

Contents

ONE

The Gentleman

"I'm sorry," the Gentleman said sincerely as he disappeared. The dust, the dusk, and the distance soon swallowed him.

It was at this time of year when we first met the Gentleman. Leaves that lay dry on the ground lifted quickly, reached in a spiral, swirled, then slowly dropped back to the ground, only to be caught up once again in a gust; this process would not end until frost glued them to the ground. The angle of the sun to the earth afforded just enough light to warm the fields. The chimneys puffed gently. The fireplaces warded off the early morning chill and late afternoon nip. The smell of wood-burning stoves baking homemade breads, pies, roasts, and every kind of fowl was constant. The smell permeated the village. This one fact told the story of our town's prosperity. Everyone was satisfied. It was a town whose Christmas lists consisted of wants, not needs.

Few living residents could remember the Great Collapse, and those who could had long ago grown weary of the ridicule attached to telling and retelling the horror stories. The bins were filled, the lofts bulged, and banks were busy. It was a wonderful time to live. The plague that had touched and taken small ones from each and every family had long since been cured. We had the best extended care facility for the advanced and mature in our entire county. No longer were there screams of unremitting pain heard in its halls. Moans were "peacefully" muffled. Pain medication was a godsend. Unpleasant odors were covered with the pungent scent of Lysol perfume. We never hurt, and, as in the case of Eddy McCracken, who fell from the highest limb of the tallest apple tree in Picketts' Orchard, even that pain was quickly extinguished by an injection into his fleshy arm.

The Fellowship Hall was the center of town. Some said it used to be a community church, but when its few remaining elderly members died, the building was left unattended and the woods began to take it back. Activities were planned from early morning until well after eleven every night. Adjacent was the public pool, the pride of the state. There was always something to do.

Our school was proud of sending 83% of its graduates to colleges, many of them prestigious. Students excelled in math and the sciences. The teachers were considered the best. They were recruited from all over the country and weren't even interviewed unless they were in the top 5% of their graduating class, won local or state awards, and were "published."

The Arts Council had no sooner finished one event when they were planning the next. Our local dramatic repertoire group presented four full-scale productions each and every year. Public services were impeccable. Potholes exposed during the day disappeared during the night. Plowing was efficient, and snowstorms gave us little reason for concern. Power outages lasted seconds, not hours or days.

The *Daily Bugle* and the *Weekly Sentinel* had little to herald or warn against. Both papers were mostly ads, reports of surrounding community family get-togethers, births, marriages, and death notices.

Our radio station was fully automated, and you could set your clock by when Johnny Mathis once again slipped into "Chances Are." Because of our geographical location, our "hill" was coveted by competing TV cable companies, who, in exchange for using it to transmit, wired everyone's home with free cable TV. Crime was virtually nonexistent. Well-paid, well-educated police officers with the latest technologies and well-lit streets and Neighborhood Watch programs—I mean real Neighborhood Watch programs—forced would-be criminals to prey on surrounding communities.

Everybody had a niche. There was no reason to be bored. Idle time was unheard of. In the summer, with the convergence of the Fair, the Triathalon and the Chautauqua, we would fall asleep in the car on our way home. Our dads wrapped our sweaty bodies in blankets and carried us limp into the house. For a split second, as we hit the bed, we were half awake, and we knew we were safe, secure, and satisfied.

Our motto, proudly emblazoned on the town limit signs, read: "Here we do unto others as we'd have them do unto us." There was never trouble with getting a neighbor's help, no fear of litigation over Good Samaritan laws. The moral law overrode minor technicalities and even major statutes.

There was a genuine concern for one anothers'
welfare. It was the law. No one contemplated its
origin. There was no need. It was merely a matter
of survival. It was practical.

I guess you could say it was a perfect town
and time. And it was—except for the "hole." And
because of that, conditions were ideal for the
Gentleman. I don't know how else to describe
him. He was a gentleman. He had the appearance
of someone special. His demeanor demanded respect. He stood six-foot-four with penetrating blue
eyes. Though not old, he had silver hair, a deep,
resonant voice that refused not to be heard. He
was charisma.

Fate had sent the Gentleman. Everything he
said directly appealed to the "hole." Members of
academia, with efficacious accents, spent faculty
meetings at the local college discussing his impact,
and the local sophists gathered downtown, continually interrupting one another's conversations
about the weather, crops, foreign cars, and the
mayor's wife, with philosophical tidbits, droppings
heard second, third, or fourth hand from the
Gentleman. The Gentleman's concepts satisfied
logic and sensibilities.

Conservatives and Liberals embraced his
teachings. He offended neither. People couldn't
get enough. They loved to hear him. They were a
"religious" people, but they longed for something
spiritual. And he provided it. It offended none
and elevated all. He called for a turn to God, a
god who demanded obedience, a god who yearned
only to be released from inside each one. As the
people matured in this faith, they all felt better
about themselves. In retrospect, this was the first
sign of trouble. Fences criss-crossed the landscape.

The courts became clogged. Litigation was the common method of reconciling differences, but never relationships. Police had no respect for each other. Rebellion among the young seemed to be an indisciplined search for an ultimate truth. Suicide among all ages was the number one cause of death. Parents could not control children. Parents could not control themselves. The longest column in the weekly papers was now "Divorces." He stayed in town for three years, then left, leaving behind rubble.

"I'm sorry," the Gentleman said sincerely.

TWO

How to Change a Society: The Role of Man and God

Great changes in a society occur subtly, seldom with fanfare. Great lasting changes occur slowly. Revolution is seldom the result of a single cataclysmic event but rather a long period of dissatisfaction.

Soil, in order to produce fruit, must be fertile and prepared. Bountiful crops are the result not so much as of the farmer or the seed but of the properly prepared soil. Changes in society are not the result of a skilled orator or a brilliant message but of a group of people anxiously receptive to change; hungry, needing to fill a void.

Today's society is fertile for the planting of the New Age seed, sowed by a wide variety of farmers; from bearded Hindu and beaded-robed gurus to handsome, charismatic speakers in the latest suit fashions, from movie stars to tea leaf readers. Ridiculed, renounced, and rejected a few years ago, they are attended to by groupies clinging to every name, nonsensical word, or prophesy. The New Age and its doctrines are not new. They

15

are merely re-clothed dogmas of the past. Ecclesiastes 1:9: "There is nothing new under the sun." Why the appeal to a repeated failure? A short look at human history provides some illuminating answers.

Historical Overview

The examination of the rise and fall of cultures reveals that each one deceived itself into the belief of its immortality. The foundational concepts and concurrent generations' re-establishment or shoring up of those foundations are usually accurate indicators of cultural longevity. Any building's stability and longevity is based primarily on its foundation. Our Constitution has survived and therefore insured unbelievable benefits based on the careful, meticulous, investigative, debate-filled mind sets that were so careful in laying the stones that became the Constitution and Bill of Rights, and each succeeding generation's acceptance and veneration of these ideals. Greece fell; Rome fell; Germany fell; Britain's empire shrank. The USSR is no longer in existence. Societal perpetuation is based not only on its founding premise and promise but also on each succeeding generation's hunger for making those ideals their own and on their willingness to sacrifice to preserve it.

Every new society, be it as vast as the Roman empire or as small as the family unit, must have a reference point, a cornerstone upon which it has been built. In the Soviet Union, it was the good of the atheistic state; in Rome the deified power of the emperor; in Greece, culture with a pantheon of gods and goddesses in ultimate fateful control; in Nazi Germany, the Aryan supremacy, and every modern attempt at establishing various communes is based on the ultimate good (God) of man.

A closer look reveals that all cultures are based on man's and/or God's (or gods') relative position in the universe. Even atheistic societies have made a decision on God's role in their society. They have chosen to exclude the traditional God and have instead inserted an alternative. Perhaps this speaks well of the innate need of man to seek God. Even without society's willing acknowledgment of it, God has had a vital role in the establishing and maintaining of every societal unit, grandiose or small. Tension exists when the relationship between God and man becomes unbalanced. Ultimately when a society collapses, the new society's success at re-emergence is once again based on its establishing a reference point upon which to build: God (god[s]) or man.

Since atheism is a religion whose supreme deity is nature or an undefined impersonal force, and the word *religion* is from Latin and means "to tie back," the question must be raised, "tied back to what or to whom? Religion is the glue designed to hold a society together and to explain the past, present, and future, i.e., to give it "meaning." This meaning determines the goals, ethics, morality, and responsibility of a culture or society.

Let's, for a moment, look at our nation's history. Some of our founders were decidedly deists. They believed in the eternal existence of God. He created all. Their theology also proposed that God, having done His work, had withdrawn Himself from the day-to-day machinations of mankind. God was a stern judge, and it was by His code that all humanity would be judged eternally. God was feared. The Puritan ethic emphasized fear of punishment rather than the present and anticipated joys of Christ's inheritance. Each new community in New England was usually precipitated by religious dissension. Slight changes in biblical hermeneutics were looked upon as doctrinal heresy. Ostracism, persecution, and witch hunts prevailed. The church and government (state) were mutually inclusive. By the time of the American Revolution, our constitutional framers were arguing and agonizing over this relationship. Even to this day, there rages the argument over the church/state relationship (i.e., the role of God vs. role of man in society).

With sanctioned separation, the whole spectrum of reference point alternatives developed. The early nineteenth century precipitated a prevailing view of the evolving "nature" of man, spurred by Darwin's theories (note: much attributed to Darwin is, in fact, not Darwinism, and even if it is to be found in his writings, it is still to be regarded as theory). It was believed that man was basically good (contrary to Catholic and Anglican views of the nature of man) and getting better. World War I shattered this illusion. Harmony based on mutual respect without a divine model proved a failure. Pessimism prevailed. The Great War ended the illusions of moral supremacy and godless grandeur. Perhaps, some argued once again, man *was* evil. Religious pendulums swing in America just as calculably as political liberal and conservative stands. Balance evades humanity.

As the country hit the Depression of the thirties, priorities reflected a value system based not on the material but on relationships, trust of neighbor and dependence upon God. Affluence followed, however, and the concept of the self-made man, the Horatio Alger story, was reflected in Hollywood and on Main Street, USA, the wide screen, and on the radio, which was soon to be replaced by the TV. A booming economy, a victory in war, the advance of technology, computerization, and landing on the moon all initiated a resurgence in the concept of man as god.

Secular humanism resulted, a moral code based on the premise that man is god, and god is good. Even some advocates of this egocentric heresy realized that morality was necessary for self preservation. "Humanism is a polite term for atheism" (James Curry, President, American Humanist Association). Secular humanism, or morality without the need of God, failed. It is over. Why do some people, especially Christians, continue to wage war against an enemy that collapsed as a result of its own deficiencies? A system based on the elevation of man and the dismissal of God must fail. Man cannot do what God can do, and God will not do what man can do. Secular humanism's failure was its denial of the innate need of man for God. Voltaire was right: "If God didn't exist, we would have to invent Him!" But He does.

Strategy and the Hidden Agenda

Voids cannot, by definition, remain. Something will fill a need; thus the birth of what is called the New Age. This is nothing more than secular humanism with a spiritual ingredient: man is god. Because the shoes of God are impossible to fill, the New Age will collapse. What we don't know is how many will be crushed in its fall.

This chapter is designed to give "the greater picture" of the New Age movement. Even the title implies patient progress. It is not static. It will not go away. It isn't a fad. Much like the inevitable advance of a glacier, so are the tentacles of this religiously heretical octopus weaving their way into every institution, from Hollywood TV productions and stars, to medicine, music, toys, the pulpits of once doctrinally sound churches, and the most dangerous arena of all—the school. The tentacles are not only in the school corridors. They have already entered the room and begun to entangle the minds of the administrators, teachers, and students in the guise of textbooks and participatory exercises. But because "it seems good to the eye, and it tastes good" (Gen. 3:6), it is invited even further into the educational setting.

These parts, or tentacles, looked at individually, seem lifeless and harmless. But that is a myopic and incorrect diagnostic perspective. All of us have been shown pictures that when viewed from up close appear to be one thing but when viewed in perspective present an altogether different picture. Such is the New Age, a mosaic of individual ingredients, harmless in themselves, that together are a recipe for poison. The price paid for not being watchful is often traumatic and lasting. Vigilance is most necessary when it seems least important. Even more dangerous is the arena in which basic principles are attacked from seemingly unrelated entities.

Seldom is it a frontal attack, that would be announcing their true intent. Basic principles are usually attacked with such an indirect methodology that even those holding the principle dear become unwitting advocates in this moral erosion. Causes well worth championing are all part of a larger battle plan, an agenda of a new morality.

This is guerilla warfare—the enemy easily recruited from a worldwide pool of dissatisfied individuals in search of ultimate truth.

What are we talking about when we say the New Age? The very fact that even New Agers disagree on a definition is a major part of the problem. To be unable to "define" the enemy is the greatest strategical ploy of all. That's why so many are caught in its web and yet are totally unaware of its dangers.

Americans are not stupid. Seldom are we easily deceived. I have always espoused the adage, "There is no such thing as a free lunch." Everything has a cost. I always enjoyed looking at the small print in various "giveaways" in newspaper ads, listening carefully to TV or radio announcements offering an unbelievable deal, to discover the "hidden cost." I developed a certain pride and silently ridiculed suckers entrapped in quick money-raising schemes. That is until last winter.

My wife and I needed a vacation. I had given 125 seminars the last year. The phone rang. The voice immediately set off my "scam" defense mechanism. I listened to the whole spiel. Not because I was going to purchase anything—I only wanted to find the "hook," expose the rip-off, and reprimand the seller. Then my salutary attention was changed to alert awareness when the person on the other end of the line offered a guaranteed, all expense, round-trip vacation to Hawaii for two. Several times I asked her if it was all expenses for "two," if the hotel was paid for, all the usual questions to ask in these "giveaways." All I could see

was a guaranteed trip for Pam and me to Hawaii
by purchasing a $300 membership. Three hun-
dred dollars! I needed a vacation, what luck! I'd
save a fortune. One month later I received the
brochure. I did win a trip to Hawaii. It did cover
all expenses for two. The hook: I had to purchase
at full price a third ticket! I am $300 poorer and
maybe a little wiser.

At this point, it is critical that we understand
that the New Age movement is not a cult. It is
more accurately defined as an occult movement.
Unfortunately, we make the improper assumption
that these words are interchangeable. They are
not. A cult group is a fringe religious group. We
often dismiss the significance of cult groups because they are usually small, wear bizarre clothing
or hair styles, and most often are self-destructive.
For these reasons, they are not always taken seriously for the true danger they represent. They
vociferously defend the Bible as authoritative but
ignore generally accepted hermeneutic rules. They
tend to focus on one aspect of biblical teaching
and then interpret other biblical principles based
on that "core" teaching. There is always a charismatic leader, living or dead, whose words or writings are "supplements" to the Bible (by which they
really mean not only equal in importance but, in
the case of conflict, superior to the Word of God).

These groups use all means of mind control,
everything from simple manipulation to outright
blackmail. In some groups, the diet consists of
high carbohydrate, low protein foods, affecting
blood sugar levels and thus the ability to reason.
Sleep deprivation is utilized. Repetitive tasks, such
as selling flowers or books on street corners or in

other public areas, are used as a means by which members might earn "salvation" (a term that each cult defines differently). People ensnared by cult groups are usually guilt ridden individuals, anxiously looking for a leader who is willing to take responsibility for meeting their daily needs.

The occult (the word means "hidden"), on the other hand, is based on direct opposition to the God of the Bible. It is egocentric, with man containing his own deity. (We will examine the specific religious tenets, or pillars, of the New Age in the next chapter.) And so it follows that those drawn to the occult are drawn to its "power." This has proven universally true. I have had young children and senior citizens (one a seventy-three-year-old wife of a police chief) express that the motivation for interest and involvement was to attain power. It is thus clear that a major distinction between cults and the occult is the profile of the person they attract.

Parts of the New Age Machine

Let's look at some individual tenets of the New Age and then "connect the dots" to see it for the monster it really is.

Just as in Christendom, there are many different types of New Age denominations. The only agreement between all these disparate groups is the acceptance of human deity and some form of reincarnation. These we will examine in chapter 3.

New Age Components

All of us have heard of the "crystal craze." Every place from high couture shops in Beverly Hills to cheap department stores in malls have crystal pendants for sale. What's the big deal? Herb

Alpert of Tijuana Brass fame reportedly has a 750-pound piece of quartz in his home. Teen-agers have tiny chips dangling from their ears.

According to some New Agers, crystals are related to human beings because both the human body and crystals contain silicon dioxide. Many readers are too young to remember the forerunner of compact disks and walkmans: the crystal radio. When a radio signal from an antenna was directed to a tiny crystal in the set, the crystal vibrated at a consistent frequency (i.e., radio frequency or channel). The energy contained within the crystal was released. The human body is solid energy waiting to be released as well. This is accomplished through vibration. Mantras, or resonant tones repeated over and over, set up the vibratory channel, thereby releasing the trapped energy (deity) within.

New Agers refer to crystals as "holy ice." Beyond crystals lies the whole realm of precious and semi-precious stones, each purporting to possess powers ranging from the curative to the financially enhancing. One catalogue states that amethyst has the power to overcome indulgences, heal, enhance psychic power, protect, provide courage and emotional love, and guarantee success. Jasper enhances beauty. Moonstone will aid in dieting. Moss agate is an excellent talisman for gardeners. A sodalite pendant heals throat problems.

How easily deceived we are! Few Christians would purchase and seek to release energy from a crystal ball, yet they proudly display its shattered pieces around their necks.

Herbs, oils, and incenses are next on the shopping lists of many New Agers. One company peddles a combination of sage and sage oil to be used in ritual cleansing and exorcism, mugwort and frankincense for protection, and jasmine mixed with wild rose petals for fertility. No self respecting astral traveler would be without Dragons' Blood resin.

Candles have magical powers as well. Various colors appeal to various powers. In satanism, the burning of red candles indicates sexual ritual, black curse, hatred, or death rituals. Botanicas, or places to purchase occult supplies, will sell candles "dressed" or specially prepared for specific needs. I recently called a botanica while on a speaking trip to California. I asked the cost of a candle dressed for the purpose of keeping police away: less than five dollars.

The supernatural realm attracts New Agers. Seances and tarot card readings to communicate with the spirit world hold to New Agers the promise of success in business and personal ventures. Late night TV hawks 1-900 numbers, putting callers in instant contact with your favorite astrologer. Whether it's crystals or the planets, nature holds the secrets to all life's dilemmas. I find it fascinating that people will consult a Ouija board to determine their future. Is not who we are tomorrow based on what we do today? A person glued to a Ouija board will be the same person tomorrow (note: Ouija comes from two words *oui*—yes in French and *ja*—yes in German; in other words, the "yes-yes" board; it will tell you whatever you want to hear).

Psychic fairs are all the rage. Along with all the attractions listed above, they provide tea leaf readings, palm readings, foot readings, cranial bump readings, and the list goes on and on. I at-

tended one of these fairs recently and spied a lone
woman seated at a table, and behind her, arrayed
on a wall, were what appeared to be randomly
spray painted T-shirts. I approached her, and she
told me that for a certain price she could "channel" a likeness (aura) of my personal spirit guide
onto a T-shirt using paint. I explained that as a
Christian my spirit guide was Jesus and His Holy
Spirit and asked how many of those she had done.
I left her with a bewildered look on her face.

Invariably, off to one side at these fairs, is a
solitary pyramid fashioned from glass rods, wooden
sticks, and even canvas tents. To be in the center
(or vortex) of such a structure is to ensure peace,
harmony, and the release of your psychic energy.
Some hold that bread suspended from the center
of the pyramid will not mold and that razor blades
will be sharpened. "Pyramid power" is in. Office
buildings are being designed in this model to insure ultimate worker productivity.

Corporations are employing New Age con-
sultants to motivate and energize employees. Self-
esteem workshops, self-awareness seminars, self-
actualization encounters, and self-awareness insti-
tutes are all focusing on an employee's discovering the real, unhindered "you within yourself." All
answers are found by introspection and self-ex-
amination. You contain all truth, and you are your
greatest enemy. When I speak to high-school
groups around the country, I ask three simple
questions: Have you ever visited a nursing home?
Did you want to? Did you feel like a better person
after you went? Invariably, the answers are yes, no,
and yes. The key to self-esteem, therefore, is not
to be found inside oneself but in the knowledge
that you are needed by someone else. In the secu-

lar arena, this is community service; in Christianity, Jesus called it servanthood, or ministry.

Channeling is all the rage, popularized by actress/dancer Shirley MacLaine, and J.Z. Knight, who channeled "Ramtha," a purported 35,000-year-old spirit. Other Hollywood notables have joined the ranks of those consulting departed spirits. Trans-channellers are the mediums through whom the spirits communicate (note: Deut. 18:10,11 states that such practices are an abomination to God).

New Agers accept a concept of eternal life, but in the form of reincarnation (see chapter 3 for an in-depth discussion of this doctrine). Not only are they interested in the future, but they are also fascinated by their past. Many feel that the trauma of physical birth has left unhealed wounds to their spirit. It is therefore necessary to go through a rebirthing process in which, with the help of a New Age therapist or practitioner, they supposedly recall the trauma and come to terms with it. One guru has stated, "It's never too late to have a happy childhood."

At the other end of the life spectrum, we have those transfixed with the death experience. This was first popularized by Raymond Moody in his book, *Life After Life*. In it, he selectively chronicles the near death experiences of men and women. They all reported similar occurrences, which included OBE's or Out-of-Body Experiences. Technically, this is referred to as autoscopic visualization, in which you see yourself (body) from the perspective of your separated soul. It is interesting that Dr. Kubler-Ross, the pioneer of thanatology, or the study of death, has recently been involved in the paranormal and reportedly has her own spirit guide, Salem.

Closely akin to this phenomena is astral projection, or the separating of the body and spirit while still alive. I have talked with people who said they did this and claimed that they could accurately report specific conditions in distant places with no other means of communication.

Another characteristic common to New Agers is a militant attitude concerning the environment. New Agers are pantheistic. That is, God is in all: you, the trees, and the rocks. Thus, all creation is to be worshipped. We as Christians can accept the concept of responsible stewardship (Gen. 2:15) but certainly not for the same reasons.

In the field of medicine, we see an interest in a holistic approach to healing. This, too, poses no problem to the Christian, except that in the New Age, the purpose of healing is to make the individual "whole" so that he can be in tune physically/psychologically with nature, thus realizing the fullness of the deity (centering) within himself.

Various relaxation techniques have the same goal. As Christians, the body is the dwelling place of His Holy Spirit (James 4:5), and we are to take good care of it. Closely akin to this is meditation with the focus to empty one's mind or exit one's body (astral project) in order to achieve peace. Meditation to the New Ager has altogether different connotations than to the Christian. It is egocentric in nature and seeks to release the "divine god" within oneself.

I meditate. Scripture admonishes us to meditate on God's Word. Prayer, a continual reminder of my relationship to God, provides the "peace that passes all understanding" (Phil. 4:7).

The same warning should be made concerning hypnosis. We are to be responsible, and in order to be such, we must be in control at all times. Guided imagery, or creative visualization, used to obtain levels of relaxation, is a potentially dangerous tool in the hands of most people, particularly authority figures when children are involved. With school personnel, it raises the question of informed consent and the risky possibility of practicing psychiatry (medicine) without a license. Lawsuits are a real potentiality.

On to the more easily recognizable elements of the New Age, wicca ("the craft of the wise") purports to be white, or good, magic. As will be demonstrated in later chapters, it is found throughout the public school curriculum. It is interesting to note that even Anton LaVey, the founder of the Church of Satan in the U.S., says that there is no difference between white (good) and black (evil) magic. American Indian shamanism is also readily found in textbooks though, like wicca, it is a recognized religion.

Yoga ("union or yoke with god") is espoused as both a relaxation technique and exercise. Any serious practitioner knows that yoga practiced without its religious significance and intent is impossible since the goal of yoga is to align oneself with the deity. Hindus believe that the goddess Shakti resides at the base of the spine. In order to achieve her purpose, she must have union with Shiva (another Hindu god). This is accomplished by allowing the force (kundalini) to rise through six chakras, or spiritual centers of energy, in the hollow of the spinal column. The seventh chakra is Shiva. This alignment of all seven chakras and the psychosexual union of Shakti and Shiva produces "oneness with god." The form of this completed kundalini is a serpent.

The New Age is largely Eastern mysticism cloaked in western terminology and adapted to Western culture. All of these "dots," or components of what is called the New Age are evident in much more subtle form in cartoons that focus on mythical creatures or witches who are portrayed as heroes or heroines. Rabid environmentalism, focusing on the worship of the created rather than the Creator, is a popular theme. Games that are blatantly occult in nature, like many of the fantasy role playing games, are of great concern. Not that long ago a fourteen-year-old I know was prepared to kill himself because, as the leader of one of these games, he believed that a young girl in a distant city died as a result of a curse he had put on her. Black metal music, echoing themes of hatred, rebellion, killing, and all manner of sorcery is available in record stores. Toys depicting evil villains as heroes are direct attacks on parental values.

The soil of dissatisfaction is fertile. It has been plowed. New Age seeds have been planted. We are yet to see the fruit of this harvest.

THREE

The Garden of Eden: New Age, Old Lie

There is a God-Shaped hole in every man's Heart.

St. Augustine

We, as Christians, live in an ideal time. Never has the field been "whiter for harvest." The mere existence and popularity of the New Age is evidence of a spiritual search of a magnitude never before seen in history. Our job description, as given in Matthew 28:19,20 ("Go therefore to all nations and make them my disciples; baptize them in the name of the Father and the Son and the Holy Spirit, and teach them to observe all that I have commanded you. I will be with you always, to the end of time."), has given us a vital role at a critical time. The indwelling of His Holy Spirit has equipped us for that unique task.

Unfortunately, the church is so preoccupied with secondary issues, that we are not visible or attractive to a spiritually starved generation. There are some who are drawn to the New Age because

31

it requires so little. The cost is minimal, but, in the
end, the allure and promise prove empty. Inferior
substitutes fail to meet the deepest needs and
longings of mankind. Sooner or later, the counter-
feit is exposed.

Have you ever had a burning desire for a
particular snack? Let's say, Twinkies. Nothing else
will do. This "attack" usually occurs at about 10:45
P.M. Although you are a mature individual in other
areas of life, you quickly dress, get into your car,
and begin the "quest." From convenience store to
convenience store, you frantically seek out those
non-nutritional nuggets of gold. Finally, the search
ends. No sooner are you reseated in your car than
crumbs decorate the front of your shirt, a cello-
phane wrapper statically clings to your sleeve, a
vanilla chemical accents your upper lip, and the
void is filled.

All of us are born with a spiritual void. This is
an innate need that only God can fill. All the
facets or manifestations of the New Age mentioned in chapter 2 are based on two presuppositions or pillars. The first: man/woman is god. The
second: reincarnation replaces the biblical concepts of death and eternal judgment. Let's examine these two pillars individually. If either proves
false, the New Age theology is one based on faulty
presuppositions, which will collapse and leave the
spiritual void unfilled.

Man as God

The New Age position on the nature of man
is clear. You are god. This is an egocentric, rather
than Christocentric, religion. As in all false pre-
mises, this one leads to false conclusions. If man is

indeed god, he/she is responsible only to self as the highest authority. The reference point for determining right and wrong is totally subjective. If this is true, each individual populating the globe answers only to himself—ultimate anarchy. The motivation for "respecting" others is merely self-preservation. The moral code is not dictated by love but by necessity: I am good to you so that you will be good to me. This is the Golden Rule without a spiritual dimension or responsibility.

There is no such thing as sin in the New Age theology. Our only failure as individuals is that we fail to realize the deity within each one of us. This is to be enlightened, a word used frequently by New Agers. Every generation has one or more people who become enlightened enough to be avatars (in Hinduism, incarnation of a god). These include Jesus, Mohammed, Gandhi, and others. They are no more god than you, but they fully realize their potential.

Thus, in this New Age, we have a polytheistic religion, one consisting of many gods. This is contrary to both the Old and New Testament teachings concerning the existence of but one God. As we examine these propositions, it is necessary to compare them to a reference point that has proven consistent, relevant, practical, and true for thousands of years. Is man God? The book of Genesis (Hebrew for "beginning") makes it clear that all that exists includes a single Creator and what He created. Any scientific model requires that this truth be incorporated into it. The names for this Creator are many: the force, a molecule, nature, only the Bible defines the origin of these attempts at explaining our existence and order in the universe. Even the classic evolutionist must honestly acknowledge that he can go back only so far and must admit that the original impetus for initiating evolutionary change is beyond his explanations.

"In the beginning, God created the heavens and the earth" (Gen. 1:1). This passage is the most powerful in recorded history. Traditional science teaches us that all that exists requires five components: time, force, action, space, and mass. Now, rereading this first sentence of God's Word, we find all five components: "In the beginning (time), God (force), created (action) the heavens (space), and the earth (mass)."

Who is this God of Genesis 1:1? Certainly not man, for man's creation is not specifically mentioned until the twenty-sixth verse of this chapter. Man is a created being, not a creator. Man has never created anything. He has merely assembled, in different proportions, what God had already placed here. And even this accomplishment is only possible by the use of the mind and dexterity God created within him. If we take away the biblical Creator God, there is no man.

After the creation of man, detailed in Genesis 3, we see clearly the hierarchy established in the relationship of man to God. Genesis 3:7 says, "The Lord God formed a human being from the dust of the ground and breathed into his nostrils the breath of life, so that he became a living creature." Not only is our origin humble (dust), but our very animation was dependent upon God's own breath. At this point man was totally dependent upon God. In verses 8 and 9, God provided shelter and sustenance, and in verses 10-14, He provided water. In verse 15 He provided work as an antidote for idleness and, in verse 18, a "suitable helpmate" to displace loneliness. Finally, and most important, He gave rules so that all these gifts could benefit man to their utmost (Gen. 3:16,17). God's laws are always for the purpose of enriching man's life and preventing unnecessary pain.

To this point, our study of Genesis might falsely indicate that all creation, including man, is equal: Genesis 1:26 reminds us that of all creation, mankind alone was created in God's image. He was also given dominion over creation (Gen. 1:28), not to be environmentally irresponsible, but to be wise stewards to insure its preservation. Man and nature are not equals, let alone, as the New Agers insist, gods. These false teachings are referred to as polytheism and pantheism, or the full nature of god in all things, animate and inanimate.

To be created in God's image is not the same as to be God. He has given us certain innate attributes that further link us closer to Him than to all other creation. These include love, a demand for justice, a desire for truth, and a reasoning mind. We might include in this list a need for establishing and maintaining a relationship with Him.

In the New Age, this is becoming enlightened or acknowledging our own deity. This is achieved by deep introspection and facilitated by vibratory chanting, yoga postures (Chakra align-ment), and ego "centered" meditation. In God's plan, our efforts at establishing a relationship fail. Instead, we accept the gift of the relationship provided only by His Son, Jesus.

Throughout history, all of man's problems can be traced to breaking the bonds of a proper relationship with God and becoming egocentric. Whenever we try to deny our dependence upon

God, we flounder and suffer. According to Romans 8:22, even nature acknowledges, in some mystical way, the sole deity of God. Only man, of all creation, has the audacity to supplant God with self.

God alone is referred to as Almighty. ("The Lord our God the Almighty reigns," says Rev. 19:6.) This word, implying dominion over all things is used ten times in the New Testament and always of God. In theological terms, this is referred to as omnipotence. Unlike man, God manifests His inexhaustible power in the exhibition of love (Job 26:13,14).

The true God is also omnipresent (fully present in all places) according to Psalms 139:7-12 and Acts 17:27. Man cannot claim this ability. His omnipresence is entirely consistent with His spiritual existence. He is unrestrained by the likes of our fleshly comprehension. The same God that hears my cries of despair hears the muffled moans of a starving child in a far distant land. The definition of God requires no less.

The true God is also omniscient, or all-knowing. What man can claim to know everything, past, present, and future? In Psalms 139:1-6, David makes it clear that God knows even his most private thoughts. Hebrews 4:13 reminds us that nothing is hidden from God. He is aware of future events according to Acts 15:18.

"All have sinned and fallen short of the glory of God" (Rom. 6:23). No man can justifiably claim the New Age tenet of sinless perfection, much less the non-existence of sin. "If we have committed no sin, we make Him out to be a liar, and His word has no place in us" (1 John 1:10). It could be convenient to ignore the reality of sin, but it doesn't change the reality of its existence. We can change its name and color coat it, or claim no responsibility for it (as in the prevalent "disease" model in psychology and counseling), but it will never go away. The fact that conscience is innate indicates the existence of not only right and wrong but responsibility in doing right. Only God can rightfully claim holiness (see Ps. 145:17, Ps. 99:3, Ps. 111:9, and 1 Sam. 2:2). Thus, only God is worthy of worship (Ps. 86:9). According to all biblical qualifications for God, man falls far short of His glory.

The first pillar, upon which the entire New Age religion rests, is without sufficient mortar. It is an illusion. Even though it is believed by adherents, it is insufficient to sustain truth. It is a lie built on a foundation of sand.

Reincarnation

The second essential pillar attempting to support New Age religion is reincarnation, or the law of rebirth. Until an individual attains avatar status or nirvana, his soul is destined to return in the form of another entity. This process continues again and again. Shirley MacLaine is a highly visible New Ager who is anxious to share her various previous incarnations.

Westerners seem willing to embrace a theology that is impersonal and in which there is no ultimate judgment. In Paul's second epistle to the church of Corinth, he made it clear: "For we must all have our lives laid open before the tribunal of Christ, where each must receive what is due to him for his conduct in the body, good or bad" (v.10). A major distinction between the Eastern, mystical concept of reincarnation and the Christian belief in resurrection is that, in Christianity, there is a definite hope. History is linear. It has a starting point, a direction, and an end. God intended man to live in eternal existence with Him. Jesus clearly stated that He was going to prepare a place for us. Paul reminds us that "to be absent from the body is to be present with the Lord" (2 Cor. 5:6-8).

Reincarnation is cyclical. How we live this (and even past) incarnation dictates our future social status. This is determined by an impersonal force and our karma (a mystic law of cause and effect that results in present and future incarnations). One escapes from the cyclical birth-rebirth process and achieves the status of nirvana, or bliss, only by works.

If we accept reincarnation and the "justice" of karma, then we accept that we are existing in our present form as the result of a previous life's works as is everyone or everything. To change this is to upset the rule of nature. This being the case, it is easy to understand the lack of compassion for the ill, the homeless, and the poor of India, for according to this view, to be helpful is to change a person's karma. How interesting that Easterners, stuck with this virtually hopeless institution, refer to it as the "prison house of the soul." Westerners grasp karma with vigor without really understanding it and grab it because it provides a continuing spiritual existence without a God who requires praise and honor.

As Christians, we realize that after this physical life we are destined to live eternally with God, not due to our works or righteousness, but as a gift of God made available by His Son's death and resurrection—God's antidote to death. It is with boldness that we can say that every Christian is always healed, either in this life, or in the next. Those Christians who find reincarnation compatible with biblical teaching do not understand that death is not to be feared and that it occurs but once (Heb. 9:27).

Several months ago, I had a heart attack and emergency quadruple bypass. As I lay on the hospital gurney and heard the doctors say, "We're losing him!" and saw them begin CPR, I had a glimpse of and felt just a little of what Jesus promised: "a peace that passes all understanding" (Phil. 4:7). How sad the New Age religion that promises nothing except a continual return to earth, and how hopeful is our faith that promises a place prepared for us in which "He will wipe every tear from their eyes! There shall be an end to death, and to mourning and crying and pain, for the old order has passed away" (Rev. 21:4).

Conclusion

The New Age succeeds or fails based on the two doctrines we have just examined. Is man God? Are we destined to continual reincarnation? Chapter 1 of Genesis deals with God's order to Eve not to eat from the tree of the knowledge of good and evil, the inevitable penalty, death, and the desire of Eve to fill a void that led to the breaking of God's prescription for peace and harmony. In her struggle with conscience, Satan responds with the first two lies in history.

Genesis 3:1-5: The serpent, which was the most cunning of all the creatures the Lord God had made, asked the woman, "Is it true that God has forbidden you to eat from any tree in the garden?"

She replied, "We may eat the fruit of any tree in the garden, except from the tree in the middle of the garden. God has forbidden us to eat the fruit of that tree or even to touch it; if we do, we shall die."

1—"Of course you will not die," said the serpent;

2—"for God knows that, as soon as you eat it, your eyes will be opened and you will be like God himself, knowing both good and evil."

Sound familiar? The first two lies are also the pillars of the New Age movement. The words of the author of Ecclesiastes ring loud and true, "There is nothing new under the sun" (Eccles. 1:9).

Satan has patience. The most effective way to influence a culture is to begin with uncluttered, malleable minds trusting any authority figure. The school has our children nearly half of their waking lives until they are 17 or 18. It has the ability to influence for good or bad far beyond any other institution in our culture. Let's now examine this powerful influence in the next chapter.

FOUR

The Classroom: How It Began

"We are faced with the paradoxical fact that education has become one of the chief obstacles to intelligence and freedom of thought."

Bertrand Russel

Do you recall the day when the educational system fell prey to liberalism? What major program set it off? Who were the leaders in the movement? Where did they come from and what was their motive? You probably don't recall, because the change was so subtle, but the answer is simple. The quiet non-threatening influence of the New Age gurus seeped into every crack of the educational system. They wove their agenda into the curriculum of public schools and changed the educational atmosphere. Their message has silently but thoroughly crept through our school doors and has been embedded into the hearts and minds of our children.

In the Beginning

The great statesman Abraham Lincoln said,

> A child is a person who is going to carry on
> what you have started. He is going to sit where
> you are sitting, and when you are gone, at-
> tend to those things which you think are im-
> portant. You may adopt all the policies you
> please, but how they are carried out depends
> on him. He will assume control of our cities,
> states, and nations. He is going to move on
> and take over your churches, schools, univer-
> sities and corporations . . . The fate of hu-
> manity is in his hands.

But will our children be capable? All over
America today you hear, "What has happened to
our schools? Why aren't students learning?"

Fifty years ago, the problems schools faced
were simple misbehaviors: talking out of turn, chew-
ing gum, making noise during class, and running
in the halls. But today we are faced with drug and
alcohol abuse, teen-pregnancy, suicide, rape, physical assault, and robbery. It is an alarming difference. From the little red schoolhouse to urban
society, we are plagued with problems of seemingly insurmountable significance. For instance,
every day in the United States

> 2,795 teen-age girls get pregnant;
> 1,106 teen-age girls have abortions;
> 372 teen-age girls have miscarriages;
> 689 babies are born to women who have had
> inadequate prenatal care;
> 719 babies are born at a low birth-weight (less
> than 5 pounds, 8 ounces);
> 67 babies die before one month of life;

105 babies die before their first birthday;

27 children die from poverty;

10 children are killed by guns;

30 children are wounded by guns;

6 teen-agers commit suicide;

135,000 children bring a gun to school;

7,742 teen-agers become sexually active;

623 teen-agers get syphilis or gonorrhea;

211 children are arrested for drug abuse;

437 children are arrested for drinking or drunken driving;

1,512 teen-agers drop out of school;

1,849 children are abused or neglected;

3,288 children run away from home;

1,629 children are in adult jails;

2,556 children are born out of wedlock;

2,989 children see their parents divorced.[1]

(Source: Children's Defense Fund, from the *Almanac of the Christian World*, Tyndale House, 1991-1992 edition)

How employable will our youth be in the future? A study done by the Southport Institute for Policy Analysis found that more than 10 million workers in small businesses have serious problems with reading, writing, mathematics, and other skills that impair job performance.[2]

Is growing up in America today dangerous for our youth? In a society where drug abuse, crime, violence, and child neglect are increasing, what are we to do? How did we get to this point?

A recent survey showed that about 87 percent of Americans profess to believe in God and that 78 percent pray at least once a week.[3] If 87 percent of the American people proclaim to be theists, then why are we seeing a valueless society?

Is it because the New Age philosophy has permeated the value system of our youth and we are now seeing the product? I believe so. From the university to the elementary school, our youth are becoming products of a false system. To understand how we allowed this system to evolve, we need to start at the beginning. Let's look at how public education started and as it is today.

Christian Education

The public school system was founded by Christians, and for three hundred years, we saw Christian morality taught to our children. In 1633, the Dutch Reformed Church set up the first public school. In 1646, Bible-believing Puritans from Massachusetts passed a bill calling for tax-supported public schools in each township of fifty or more families. Many of these teachers were ministers, and the church in many cases served as the one-room schoolhouse.

Before and after our independence, public schools were teaching biblical morality. One of the nineteenth century textbooks used was Noah Webster's *Bluebacked Speller*, a book that emphasized phonics and character building. Before students began a lesson in the *Speller,* they recited this prayer:

No man may put off the law of God;
My joy is in His law all the day,
O may I not go in the way of sin.
Let me not go in the way of ill men.

On 12 December 1820, in Plymouth, Massachusetts, Daniel Webster said, "Whatever makes men good Christians makes them good citizens."

He held a deep commitment to biblical truths being the cornerstone of a strong moral character.

Another nineteenth century textbook series that sold over 10 million copies was the *McGuffey Readers*, written by a Presbyterian minister and taught for three generations. These biblically based readers told stories of the Pilgrims, George Washington, and other leaders, all strong role models.

America's universities and colleges were started by Christians. Harvard was founded by Congregationalists in 1636, William and Mary by Anglicans in 1693, Yale by Congregationalists in 1701, Princeton by Presbyterians in 1746, Columbia by Anglicans in 1754, Brown by Baptists in 1765, Rutgers by the Dutch Reformed in 1766, and Dartmouth by Congregationalists in 1770. The last five were born out of the Great Awakening revivals that preceded the fight for independence.

Today the influence of Christian education is not seen in the public schools. The 1962 Supreme Court ruling banning prayer from public schools was the beginning of the end of this value system. Forty years ago the predominant biblically based values were evident in the life of Western culture. Their removal has caused our culture to develop a "new morality" based on changing social attitudes.

Maybe that is the reason for many condoning the independent woman of the nineties having an illegitimate child. The new reasoning has it that it's her business, no one else's. What about the "wilding" riot recently in a large city? The media called it a wake-up call to America on the racial disharmony in our country. In other words, if disagreement leads to looting, then looting, murder, and arson are acceptable. I disagree. These events show systems that failed, systems where racial disharmony, family dysfunction, and educational failures have reached a climax. All are products of various value systems whose foundations have paved the way for the New Age.

The Failed Social System

Educator John Dewey, who wrote the *Humanist Manifestoes* I and II and others, laid the foundation for Humanist thought in public education; today, it is carried out by liberals and their organizations. Notice the similarities in the two philosophies of New Age and secular humanism.

The similarities are frightening, but worse is knowing that our children are learning these philosophies every day. Is it any wonder that children reject the values of their parents?

Professor Terry Moe of Stanford University and John Chubb, a fellow at the Brookings Institute, defined the problem well:

> Schools will be directed to pursue academic excellence, but without making any value judgments; they will be directed to teach sex education, but without taking a stand on contraception or abortion. They must make everyone happy by being all things to all people, just as politicians try to do.[4]

Humanist Philosophy

1. Holding an organic view of life, humanists reject the traditional dualism of mind and body.

2. As non-theists, humanists begin with humans, not God, nature, not deity. No

New Age Philosophy

1. The external word and consciousness are one and the same.

2. We are all God, so we are God.

deity will save us; we must save ourselves.

3. Humanists believe that man is part of nature and that he emerged as a result of a continuous process.

4. Religious humanists consider the complete realization of human personality to be the end of man's life and seek its development and fulfillment in the here and now.[5]

3. Life is for self evaluating purposes karma and reincarnation are key elements in this.

4. Awareness of the true self within leads to the mastery of one's own reality.[6]

As a classroom teacher, I can attest that this philosophy, which has trained America's youth to deny God, has filtered into textbooks, in-service training, university training, supplemental materials, and teachers unions disguised as progressive education.

John Dunphy stated in *The Humanist* magazine:

> I am convinced that the battle for humankind's future must be waged and won in the public school classroom by teachers who correctly perceive their role as the proselytizers of a new Faith; a religion of humanity that recognizes and respects the spark of what the theologians call divinity in every human being. Those teachers must embody the same selfless dedication as the most rabid fundamentalist preachers, for they will be ministers of another sort, utilizing a classroom instead of a pulpit to convey humanist values in what-

ever subject they teach, regardless of the educational level—pre-school, day care or a large state university. The classroom must and will become an arena of conflict between the old and the new—the rotting corpse of Christianity, together with all its adjacent evils and misery, and the new faith of humanism, resplendent in its promise of a world in which the never-realized Christian ideal of 'love thy neighbor' will finally be achieved.[7]

Without this humanistic foundation firmly in place, the New Age philosophy could not have been so subtly placed into the educational agenda. Once all morals, values, and religion are removed from children's minds, it is much easier to sell them on another way of thinking, a way of thinking that can change a country.

The Beginning of the End

The social system that has the greatest impact on Americans today is that of the public schools. The institution where 180 days, 7 hours a day, students learn, interact, and respond to teachers.

One thirty-two-year veteran in the public schools is a special education teacher who works with students 180 days out of the year. Her passion for teaching reached beyond the classroom when she discovered her teachers' union supported liberal positions.

This is an educational union that should be supporting education, not . . .

• federally day care
• abortion on demand
• reproductive rights

- legitimizing homosexuality as an acceptable alternative lifestyle
- leftist causes around the globe[8]

To her dismay, they opposed home schooling, prayer, and parental involvement. Discovering this, she immediately got involved in the next union convention. She didn't just go and observe; she spoke to the entire convention, expressing her concerns on positions the union was taking.

She is not alone in her concerns. The liberal agenda is not what all members believe. They would rather see their unions involved in educational issues, not the above causes plus three- and four-year-olds in kindergarten; reduced arms; global education; world peace; world court; and values clarification.

With 27 million, or one out of twenty-five, American adults functionally illiterate, with reading skills below the *eighth* grade level, why do teachers' unions get involved in the liberal National Endowment for the Arts, international consumer protection, nuclear freeze reduction, etc.[9] Aren't they supposed to be supporting educational issues?

Schools do have the greatest impact on our youth today, and the union's philosophies impact your child's program. In the next two chapters, you will see the impact of such union thinking, how their philosophies are rooted in the New Age, and then come to fruition in your child's curriculum.

FIVE

The Curriculum and Textbook Content

The direction in which education starts a man will determine his future life.

Plato

Many parents and teachers are not aware of how New Age concepts enter school curricula. Most recall being taught the basics: reading, writing, spelling, history, science, geography, English, and math, but not a specific subject on New Age. The reason is that New Age is not taught as a subject. It's integrated into the curriculum through textbooks, short stories, games, supplemental materials, and guided activity and can be presented through concepts, ideas, and teaching strategies. The specific content isn't planned; it evolves through these channels.

Through various teaching activities, children can learn spells, chants, practice magic, and role play such as supernatural characters. Or in a health, family living, or social studies class, they can come to deny the values you taught them and learn to form their own values based on their needs, desires, and circumstances. And if they are assigned a book report for a class project, they can read a book on Buddhism, Indian religions, or Greek mythology, but not Christianity.

The *McGuffey Readers*, which taught millions of children to read, have been replaced with textbooks that instill fear, violence, and New Age themes. From channeling to crystals to positive imaging, New Age concepts have replaced the Christian values that were once openly taught in textbooks and other materials. Throughout this chapter, you will see how a curriculum is developed and the various ways New Age concepts seep in and spill out.

Curriculum Development

When teachers teach, they need a plan. They need to know where they are going and how to get there. School curriculum models provide this. The Curriculum Development Task Force of the National Institute of Education defines a curriculum to be "the intended outcomes of instruction (i.e., all knowledge, abilities, skills, attitudes, values, behaviors, and other attributes intended for acquisition by learners)."[1] Or, in simple terms, "a plan for providing sets of learning opportunities for a person to be educated."[2]

But the questions are, "Who designs the plan?" and "Who helps develop the plan?" You might think it begins with the classroom teacher. It doesn't. It begins at the top.

Curriculum ideas are born years before they reach the classroom. Teachers have some input, but there are three phases of development. In phase 1, all five agencies, textbook publishers, national volunteer agencies, university and accrediting systems, and federal and state government, develop their own plan that assists the teacher in curriculum development. Phase 2 can mandate a curriculum to be taught in schools and development, and phase 3 utilizes these plans in formulating a specific curriculum in the school.

Textbook Publishers

The agency with the most input into curriculum content has always been the textbook publishers. For years, they have decided what the students will learn and, indirectly, the method of instruction. The "house editors" are the people who write and research the texts and have primary control of the content. Kirst and Walker stated the position of the textbook in schools:

> Who supplies decision alternatives to local schools? Until ten years ago, the unequivocal answer to this question would have been "textbook publishers." But a lot has happened in the interim. Textbook publishing has become a part of an enlarged education industry which provides all sorts of printed, electronic, and mechanical devices for classroom use. Also, the federal government, private foundations, and various non-profit organizations of scholars, teachers, and laymen have taken a more active role in producing curriculum materials. Nevertheless, the textbook is undoubtedly still the most widely used piece of educational technology, and textbook publishers are still the most powerful influences on curriculum.[3]

National Volunteer Agencies

Textbook publishers may be a powerful influence on curriculum content, but next in line are the national volunteer agencies. These agencies have their own agenda, which they publish in books, pamphlets, articles, or newsletters and distribute these to teachers, administrators, and curriculum directors through mass mailings, workshops, seminars, or in-service/training. Their goals and philosophies are taken seriously by members in their organizations. Various organizations offering material for consideration in curriculum planning include, but are not limited to

· the National Education Association (NEA),
· the state education association,
· the National Department of Education (NDE),
· the state department of education,
· professional associations (mathematics, science, English, special education associations, etc.),
· the Joint Council on Economic Education,
· the American Association for Health, and
· the Education Development Center.

These are just a sampling of associations that contribute to curriculum development. Other agencies that submit their programs for consideration have a specific agenda. For instance:

> drug and alcohol abuse, human sexuality programs, environmental concerns, vocational education programs, sex education programs, self-esteem programs.

These programs are usually presented at teacher workshops, seminars, or in-service/training. These organizations began setting goals and plans for curriculum material in the early 1920s to aid the local teacher, curriculum committee, and state curriculum committees in developing a concise and useable plan for classroom use.

University and Accrediting Agencies

The university input into the curriculum is much different than that of textbook publishers or national volunteer organizations. They do not publish booklets or articles but set admission requirements, author textbooks, set accreditation standards for schools, and make formal announcements for class offerings and the content the student will study.

For the most part, universities set the standards of knowledge that should be required of a student. Because of this, they indirectly control the curriculum in the secondary schools, not through the writing of specific plans, but through the standards they set. On occasion, professors do contribute to textbook authorship, but this is rare; in-house editors are the primary writers.

Federal and State Government

The federal government does play a major role in curriculum development through constitutional and statutory law and various Supreme Court decisions. These decisions can mandate laws that result in curriculum changes and content.

In 1963, an explosion of federal grants swept across our country. These grants provided financial assistance to schools that participated in a specific plan. National Reading Improvement Programs, Head Start, and the National School Lunch Act are some of the grant programs that played a major role in the evolution of the school curriculum. Additionally, state government and state agencies contribute plans through provisions in state constitutions; enactment of statutory laws; court decisions; and powers granted state department/ state boards of education, such as (1) legal and regulatory powers, (2) the accreditation/standardization of schools, (3) selection of textbooks and instructional materials, (4) issuance of curriculum syllabi and guides, and (5) competency examinations.[4]

All the agencies in phase 1 contribute in some way to the makeup of the curriculum content. The last agency that plays a major role before the curriculum enters the classroom is the local school district. Curriculum development in a local school system is controlled by the school board, the superintendent, and the curriculum director. Their plans are presented to teachers in workshops or curriculum committee meetings.

From phase 1, the teacher may use a curriculum guide from one or more agencies, or he may take parts of a curriculum guide and adapt it to his teaching situation. If a teacher writes his own curriculum, he studies the various guides and culls the best information to integrate within his curriculum design.

Here is an example of how curriculum development in a local school system would look: The curriculum director asks teachers, parents, or administrators to be part of a curriculum committee. This committee sets goals and objectives and selects a subcommittee to begin new curriculum writing or updating previous curricula. The subcommittee writes the program. Once the program is written, it is sent back to the original curriculum committee for review. The curriculum committee presents the program to the curriculum council for review, and then they submit the report to the superintendent. The superintendent and curriculum director present the program to the school board for acceptance.

After acceptance by the school board, the new curriculum reaches the classroom teacher. Under the direction of the curriculum director, the teachers, principals, and department heads are in-serviced and trained in the new program. After the in-service, the teachers implement the program in their respective classrooms.

The remaining parts of this chapter will demonstrate how New Age concepts are put into the curriculum and what you can do about it.

Curriculum Make-Up

On a quiet mid-winter night, eighteen senior high-school girls from a psychology class, along with three chaperones, camped inside a newly refurbished grand opera house in Oshkosh, Wisconsin. You might think the girls were going to study the architecture of the historic building, or possibly reenact past stage performances. No, the girls were to look for supernatural happenings. In the newspaper, their mission was described thus: "Maybe you could call it ghost hunting."[5]

The girls didn't get much sleep that night because they were contacting spirits and looking for ghosts and images. One girl reported that she was the only one to see an image but said others could feel a presence. In case they became bored, their tarot cards and Ouija board were close at hand; and the teacher and students spent hours sharing ghost stories during the night.

This is an example of how New Age concepts enter the schools. Now ask yourself these questions: (1) How did these students get to the point of being convinced to go ghost hunting? (2) Why did the parents let them go? (3) Why wasn't the community up in arms over this blatant, anti-Christian event?

In the past ten years, students have been inundated with programs that contain New Age concepts. From kindergarten to senior high, programs have touched upon various forms of New Age concepts. Some of the terms that carry the New Age themes in the curriculum include:

success imagery	quieting reflex
creative visualization	mind control
stress management	guided meditation
biofeedback	zen imaging
consciousness	imagery conditioning
focused imagination	imagery guides
confluent education	holistic health
master	spirit guide
inner guide	psychic helpers
relation rainbow	psychic workshop
psychic light advisors	magic circles
astral plane	white light
alpha state	hypnosis
psychic healing	psychokinesis
yoga	transcendental
out of body experience	meditation[6]

Today, students have learned to accept these concepts. Wouldn't you, if from kindergarten to senior high school you were taught these in various courses, which used a variety of teaching techniques, by instructors whom you trust? In 1980, New Age promoter Marilyn Ferguson stated: "Because of its power for social healing and awakening, they (public educators) conspire to bring the philosophy into the classroom at every grade . . ."[7]

Marilyn Ferguson is right. It is entering the schools in the following four ways:

1. psychological curriculum,
2. specific New Age techniques,
3. specific New Age programs, and
4. various New Age theme materials.

Psychological Curriculum

The psychological curriculum is an excellent vehicle for the tenets of the New Age, because it is based upon the behavioral and emotional makeup of a child. Many educators feel they can meet the needs of a child through this channel rather than through the cognitive route. When a teacher is zeroing in on such things as: how a student values himself and others; the makeup of his self-concept, power, and connectiveness; how a child perceives himself and others; and his self-identity, the teacher feels he is teaching the whole child.[8] But what he is really doing is *changing* the value system of that child. According to Max Birnbaum, affective education began thirty years ago:

> During the 1960's, public education discovered emotions. Cognitive learning and skill training, the traditional components of education, no longer satisfied the needs of a generation that had experienced the civil rights revolt, the widening generation gap, the increasing confusion of teachers, administra-

tors, and school board members about ends
and means in education. The result was a
growing interest in various approaches to affective learning *that assign to the emotional fac-
tor in education a role as important as–or perhaps
more important than–the traditional substantive
content and skills*.(emphasis added)[9]

And Alfred Alschuer backs this up:

At the frontier of psychology and education,
a new movement is emerging that attempts to
promote psychological growth directly
through educational courses. Psychologists are
shifting their attention away from remedial
help for the mentally ill to the goal of en-
hanced human potential in normal individuals. Educators, on the other hand, are beginning to accept these courses along with the
unique content and pedagogy as appropriate
for schools.[10]

With the switch from the cognitive curriculum to the affective curriculum comes a change in
principles, the foundation upon which curriculum
lies. Citizens for Excellence in Education (CEE)
stated that eight of the most important beliefs
espoused and taught in an affective curriculum
are:

1. the meaning of life lies in subjective experience;

2. self-interest is and should be the foundation for all moral decisions;

3. the teacher should be both child advocate
and therapist;

4. problem-solving through the application of
moral relativism should be encouraged;

5. teaching by facilitation, giving no knowledge or opinions, should be the norm;

6. children are capable of making sophisticated judgments;

7. peer group pressure should be more influential in establishing values than are home, school or church values;

8. Commitment to a "clinical-therapeutic" education approach should be stressed.[11]

These principles can be taught in a curriculum through basic skills, focusing on the strengths of a learner, or through the group inquiry method. Whatever method is used, the affective curriculum changes the character, values, and behavior of students.

In 1991, the Gablers of Texas did a study on the four different types of brain waves and compared them to educational achievement. They found that

beta waves occur when a person is alert and concentrating (measured at 14 to 30 hertz cycles per second—very fast);

alpha waves occur when a person is relaxed or has his mind cleared (measured at 8 to 13 hertz—slow);

theta waves occur just before a person goes to sleep; some sources claim these occur during an altered state of consciousness (4 to 7 hertz—slower);

delta waves occur during sleep (1/2 to 3 hertz—slowest).

Their conclusion: The faster the brain waves, the more alert a person is; the slower the brain waves, the less the mind is coping with the real world. Assuming that education requires mental

activity (beta waves), classroom exercises which
suppress beta waves and encourage alpha waves
are not educational.[12] I hope many parents are
asking, "Why are the schools focusing on the affective curriculum and leaving the cognitive behind?" In chapter 7, you will learn strategies for
combating this movement.

Specific Teaching Techniques

Specific teaching techniques, such as role playing, cooperative learning, and meditation are used
to lead students to accept something foreign. In
cooperative learning, students learn how to be
interdependent. This technique is used in many
classes under the umbrella of "helping students
learn how to get along with one another." But
what they are really teaching is anti-competition
and anti-individualism. According to New Age be-
lievers, the success of a global community is based
upon its interdependence.

Role playing is another avenue for teaching
interdependence, changing personality traits or
values, and increasing empathy for another
person's situation. By guiding students through a
very simple process, teachers can alter the students' value systems by peer pressure or questioning techniques. Using the "alter ego" technique, a
student would stand behind the main character
and whisper unspoken thoughts and feelings. This
pressures a student to believe in an alternate belief system, or face rejection by his peers. Only a
strong believer could submit to such pressure from
peers. And this method goes hand-in-hand with
the inquiry method. Students are expected to learn
to formulate their own problems and seek solu-

tions to these problems and do this all "on their own." The teacher acts as a "guide" or "facilitator," not as the traditional teacher who gives out knowledge.

It is hard to believe that meditation would be a teaching technique used in schools, but unfortunately it is. Ten-year-old Jason Newkirk from Lansing, Michigan, knows enough about meditation and therapy to last a lifetime. He was subjected to this and is psychologically damaged because of dangerous therapy sessions with his school counselor.[13]

Unfortunately Jason's experience is not isolated. Guided fantasy is another technique that is a form of meditation. The schools do not call it meditation because it would be associated with the teachings of Eastern religions. They disguise it as "visualization" and "relaxation" techniques. However, the students use the same techniques as in meditation: first, they relax; second, they close their eyes; third, the teacher guides them through an experience; and last, they are asked to visualize that experience. This type of activity opens the door for children to seek out and be receptive to occult activity and Eastern religions.

Parents need to be aware of these techniques so that they can discern if they are being used in their children's classes.

Specific Programs

During the past thirty years, the psychological/affective curriculum invaded our schools with zeal. Today our concern needs to focus on various programs that carry the New Age theme. Some programs present more New Age concepts than others. A survey of "Impressions," a reading series by Holt, Rhinehart and Winston of Canada, and now Harcourt Brace Javanovich, found the books to contain:

> violence, degradation and death in 27% of the books; negativity and despair in 27% of the books; witchcraft, magic, or animism in 22% of the books; bizarre or unusual illustrations in 38% of the books; and sorcery and witchcraft in 52% of the reading selections.[14]

An example of the amount of violence and death is depicted in a "fifth" grade poem:

> "He's behind her!"
> chorused the children
> but the warning came too late.
>
> The monster leaped forward
> and fastening its teeth into his neck,
> tore off the head.
>
> The body fell to the floor
> "More!" cried the children
> "More!" "More!" "More!"[15]

Third grade children are being subjected to stories that show mutilation:

> In a nearby village lived a great chief who had three daughters. The youngest of the daughters was very beautiful and sweet-tempered and was loved by everyone. Her sisters were jealous of her and treated her cruelly . . . They took coals from the fire and burned her face so she would have scars. The young girl did not complain, but went about her work as usual.[16]

Fourth grade students read about sorceress

imagery in stories printed in the U.S.-Canadian version but deleted from the U.S. Calgary version:

> The sorceress begins
> her evil toil. She
> stirs her vat of filth
> and fat and sees it
> seethe and boil.
>
> Midst hellish smells
> she whispers spells
> and does a deadly dance,
> with words of death
> upon her breath
> she slips into a trance.
>
> Higher, higher
> burns her fire,
> distant is her voice,
> and Hades' hold takes one more soul
> as demons there rejoice.
>
> In flowing dress
> the sorceress
> falls swooning to the floor
> her brew grows cold,
> her tale is told,
> her victim lives no more.[17]

This reading series is marketed in all fifty states, and parents from California to Washington are protesting. Police officer Thomas C. Jensen of California said, "I work closely with people who are involved in reports of ritualistic crime, and when children are desensitized, it is easier for them to move into that realm."[18] He went on to say that he felt this reading material would affect them later in life, and increase criminal as activity.

Thomas Jensen is concerned, and so are parents. They don't want their children subjected to

occult themes, then experimenting with more
occult activities. Some parents are writing directly
to the textbook publisher explaining their concerns. (The address is Peter Jovanovich, 6277 Sea
Harbor Drive, Orlando, FL 32887; the phone number is 407-345-2000.)

Another program that is marketed in health
classes, self-esteem, and drug education programs
is Quest International. "Skills for Adolescence"
and "Skills for Living" are the two programs produced by Quest. In 1984, Howard Kirschenbaum,
speaking to the annual convention of the Association for Supervision and Curriculum Development
said: "We have a program called the Quest
program . . . They hired myself and Barbara Glaser
to write a 400-page curriculum . . . It's a humanistic education curriculum. Rick Little, director
of it . . . thinks of it as a curriculum designed to
enhance students' self-esteem . . . It has lots of
values clarification in it . . . lots of communication skills . . . lots of self-talk . . . It's, I think you
know, a really fine synthesis of a live humanistic
education" (From Howard Kirschenbaum, "Humanistic Education: What Have We Learned in 20
Years?" [1,p.5][19]).

Professor W.R. Coulson, in a memo to the
Federal Drug Education Curricula Panel, refers to
Quest in this manner: "This humanistic education, experimental education, whatever we may
call it, is today's most commonly called 'affective
education,' with Quest the best known pack-ager."[20]

The program is designed to enhance a child's
self-esteem. It uses a non-directive approach to
teaching, telling children that their parents' values
are just one set of values they might choose when

selecting their values. Children are told there are no right answers to problems. They should select from many "alternatives" when selecting their values. Teachers are to be "guides" or "facilitators" of learning. They cannot tell a student what is right or wrong. At this young age, students are expected to make decisions based on their own experiences and not listen solely to any advise from parents, teachers, or peers.

The curriculum is saturated with values clarification, positive mental attitude, Eastern mysticism, New Age, and other concepts.[21]

A *Washington Times* article stated, "Quest tells children that they have a right to make their own decisions about whether to do drugs."[22] They make the decision, and then become responsible for the decision according to the experts. Since this is a non-directive program, teachers are not allowed to tell them that drugs are harmful, dangerous, or illegal. (For more information on Quest, write: The Mel Gablers, P.O. Box 7518, Longview, TX 75607-7518.)

Minor Programs

According to researchers, "thinking skills" are developed to improve effective thinking or to remediate deficient cognitive processes. If that is the case, then why do many programs use affective techniques such as "visualization," "energy control," "focusing," or "deep processing" in their programs? Do these New Age concepts belong in a thinking program? One program, "Tactics," which uses many of these techniques, described the following teaching activity: All the students must learn how to control their own energy. They learn how

to raise or lower their energy level and how to
create energy when there isn't any. An example
might be to take short breaths to increase energy
and slow deep breaths to lower energy.[23]

In another exercise, students are told to relax
and to look at the ceiling and focus on a spot.
From this exercise, they are to create some meaning they find in the spot. This activity is not teaching children how to think, but how to induce self-
hypnosis. The New Age concept of hypnosis tells
you to focus on an object, which can be a spot on
the ceiling, a candle, a flame, anything that can
induce a hypnotic effect. The same techniques of
deep, slow breaths, and a relaxed position are all
described.

Another program that is targeting the "at risk"
child is "Outcome Based Education." According
to Kathy Robinson of the Pennsylvania Coalition
for Academic Excellence, the regulations for "Outcome Based Education" would eliminate the traditional content-based education requiring students
to earn credits and demonstrate mastery in specific subjects.[24] The new outcomes would be "politically correct social concepts: global citizenship,
acceptance of homosexuality, self-esteem, adapt-
ability to change, higher order thought, ethical
standards, and acceptance of others." And according to David Campbell, a school reforms expert,

> The days of "chalk and talk" teaching should
> be long gone. Teachers can no longer suc-
> ceed by doing a stand-up routine in front of a
> classroom.
>
> We don't want teachers passing on informa-
> tion. We want mentors, guides, coaches, or-
> chestrators of classroom activities.

> The tools now are not textbooks, he said. I'd like to wipe them out. If you are a good teacher you don't need a textbook.[25]

He goes on to say, "If you aren't going to exploit it and be on the cutting edge, you're finished."[26] His harsh statement will rattle some cages.

Curriculum programs aren't the only areas in which to watch for New Age concepts. New Age concepts can be brought into any class. Social studies is a prime target. A recent curriculum guide told teachers that the old way of planning a guide using the following terms had to go: scientific, urbanized, mass produced, competitive, analytic, nationalistic, growth-oriented, and secular society. They would be replaced with newer in-tune concepts: service-oriented, collaborative, planetary, spiritual, holistic, and future-looking. This doesn't sound like a social studies curriculum, but the format for a religion.

Through the social studies department, the new "global" education is being promoted. Global education does not promote competition, a concept Americans value, but interdependence, where we depend on others, and other countries, for our survival. With globalism, you answer to a world court and no longer believe in nationalism. No longer will students believe in patriotism. No longer will they honor our flag. Instead, they'll learn to construct a flag that they "feel" is appropriate and "politically correct."

Another area parents need to watch is the "advisor" and "advisee" programs being incorporated into schools. These programs are not under the direction of a school counselor; every teacher is to become the "advisor." For the first half-hour of the day, teachers work on affective skill development with children. Concepts range from: getting along with others, decision making, values clarification, relaxation techniques, understanding others (in which homosexuality, for instance, is okay), and more. Teachers have a captive audience, and parents have no idea that their child is receiving a therapy session.

Another area where your child may receive a "free" therapy session is through a self-esteem program. Rev. Steve Aiken of Lansdale, Pennsylvania, studied various programs and found

> self-esteem programs address and incorporate psychological techniques that teachers and counselors are not qualified or licensed to teach; many programs use hypnosis, meditation, Buddhist and Hindu religions, guided imagery/visualization, and positive confession.[27]

In the program "Pumsy in Pursuit of Excellence," Rev. Aiken discovered that

> it claims to provide coping skills for children, but instead offers manipulations of the mind; parts of the curriculum are an affront to parental authority;
>
> it discourages open communication between parents and children;
> introduces Buddhism and Hinduism to children;
>
> hypnotic techniques are used; it promotes selfishness.[28]

Check to see if any of these materials or concepts are used in your school district. If they are, use the suggestions in chapter 7 to eliminate them from the hallways of your schools.

Various Materials

If New Age concepts were limited to only the programs described so far in this book, you might not be too alarmed. But when you see how they have saturated the publishing industry and infiltrated almost every educational avenue, your alarm bells will be ringing. To see how New Age has taken over in the classroom, a listing of publishers and materials are found below.

In a 1992 *Scholastic* catalogue, teachers can buy a "Cooperative Learning: Getting Started Kit," which contains teaching strategies for creating positive interdependence and individual accountability.[29]

In a 1992 *Avon Book* catalogue for children and young adults, teachers can buy the following books:

1. *Fifth Grade Magic*, about a fairygod mother that is full of magical spells;

2. *The Dream Book*, which tells the story of two young girls that have "connected dreams" that help find the girls' father;

3. *Eddie's Blue-Winged Dragon*, in which little Eddie buys a brass dragon that has magical powers;

4. *Good-Bye Pink Pig*, in which a pink quartz miniature pig has strange powers;

5. fifth grade monster books that are "loaded" with New Age graphics;

6. *How to Find a Ghost*, ten sure-fire ways to find a ghost for children 8-12.[30]

In a 1991 *Educational Paperbacks* catalogue for kindergarten, elementary, middle and highschool:

1. *Teeny Witch*, series for children—books on
   the adventures of witches;

2. *Magic Crystal*, a book for children that shows
   how to use magic;

3. *Jeffrey and the Third and Fourth Grade Ghost*,
   a book that makes ghosts seem real;

4. *Norman Bridwell's Witch*, a series of books
   about witches in childrens' lives;

5. For young adults, the book, *Healing
   Visualization: Creating Health Through
   Imagery*.

And if they want to read more, *Beyond
Supernature: A New Natural History of the Supernatural; The Complete Crystal Guide Book; Existen-
tialism from Dostoevsky to Sartre; Linda Goodman's
Sun Signs; Seth; and Dreams and Projection of Consciousness*. [31]

The *Trillium Press* catalogue is saturated with
New Age themes and graphics. Story visualization
is seen in grammar exercises, play writing, and
punctuation skills. "Social Concept and Affective
Development Cards" for primary school children
teach the following concepts: imagine/daydream,
pretend, death, and dying. "Reading Through
Imagery" reading activities is loaded with guided
and non-guided imagery exercises for a reading
program.

Or, if you run out of ideas, pick up the book
200 Ways of Using Imagery in the Classroom. It will
show you how to use guided fantasy with your
remedial students. In secondary classes, there is
Enhancing Writing Through Imagery, a creative
writing book for teaching "guided fantasy,"
"relaxation," and explaining what happens to the

body during imagery. And to build thinking skills we have the "Muscles of the Mind" program for pre-school children to adults, another program that advances the "visualization concept," "imagery," and the "human potential movement."[32]

I touched upon four catalogues, and there are hundreds out there that have as much or more of the New Age theme in them.

Throughout the course of the school year, teachers receive "educational catalogues." Department heads and "specialists" use these catalogues to order materials. Because of a lack of time, salesmen for the catalogue company, or the curriculum director, usually has the primary input in this selection. It would be interesting if parents were to receive these catalogues, analyze the materials, and present this information to teachers, since it is their children that are using the materials.

Curriculum Evaluation

Now that you know how a curriculum is developed and what New Age concepts to look for, your last step is to evaluate the curriculum and take action.

The first step is to ask the curriculum director for the policy on the curriculum. Your school district will have a "plan" for the program you are looking into (health, reading, English, social studies, etc.) Goals, objectives, and sequences of instruction are designed for each subject. Ask to see:

1. the statement of the school district's written policy;
2. the date the curriculum was developed;
3. the philosophy statement;

4. responsibilities for people who are involved in the course;

5. what staff were involved in writing this course;

6. whether or not parents were involved in writing this course;

7. the goals, purpose, and sequence of content;

8. whether or not people are qualified to teach this;

9. whether or not the goals and objective line-up with the federal and state guidelines;

10. what methods of instruction will be used;

11. what materials will be used; and

12. how will the students be evaluated.

Evaluating curriculum programs can be less complicated when following these steps. It's an enormous job, but one that is necessary for the survival of our children.

After you have the information, use it to create change. Dr. Bob Simonds, the president of the National Association of Christian Educators (NACE) and Citizens for Excellence in Education (CEE), recommends five steps for changing curricula in schools:

1. Assess the situation: What type of situation do you have? To what do you object? Do you have reliable information? Do you have strong support or opposition? Do you have respected people from the community behind you? Do school board members support you? What is the rationale of the curriculum? Are you trying to fill a need?

2. Write out three or four objections to the curriculum. Have a short, specific report of two pages.

3. Analyze what you have written. Before you rush off and present the report to the board, let your pastor, friends, and educators read it. Ask them for their opinion. You want to be realistic and have the problem assessed accurately.

4. Report your findings. First, talk to the teacher about your findings. Be gracious and polite; he may not know about New Age concepts. If you are not successful here, go see the principal, then the superintendent, and, last, the school board. During all these meetings, be relaxed and poised. Try to be the example that many people can copy.

Curriculum selection is a key area that parents need to be involved in to save the minds and hearts of our children. Parents who are involved can inform the teacher. Abraham Lincoln, who believed in people, said: "If given the truth, they can be depended upon to meet any crisis. The great point is to bring them the real facts."

That is our task today. To bring the facts to teachers so they can see what is "really" behind curriculum content.

SIX

A New "No" Values System

"I believe the lawless social anarchy which we saw (in the Los Angeles riots) is directly related to the breakdown of family structure, personal responsibility and social order in too many areas of our society."

And further, "If we don't succeed in addressing these fundamental problems, and in restoring basic values, any attempt to fix what's broken will fail. . .

"We are, in large measure, reaping the whirlwind of decades of changes in social mores," said Vice-President Dan Quayle at a speech to the Commonwealth Club of California on May 19, 1992.[1]

What is the reason for the "lawless social anarchy"? For decades American children learned the sound values of honesty, kindness, integrity, service, and respect. Values that parents instilled in their children by example and biblical lessons. But, ever since the public schools assumed the role of the "values provider," the moral decline in our children has increased at an alarming rate.

Yes, Vice-President Quayle, we do have a problem—and a large part of that problem started two
decades ago with the teaching of "values clarification" and the "Kohlberg" theory. This is a deliber-
ate attempt to teach children that all moral judge-
ments are equally valid.

Values Clarification

At a recent drug and alcohol training semi-
nar, the instructors recommended the following
reading be used with junior or senior high-school
students to introduce them to "Values Clarification." The participants were asked to read the
following story, "Alligator River." A group activity
and discussion would follow.

> As most stories begin...Once upon a time,
> there was a river that was practically overflow-
> ing with alligators. As you may have guessed,
> it was called Alligator River. A girl named
> Abigail lived on the west bank of the river.
> Her boyfriend, Greg, lived on the opposite
> bank. Abigail and Greg were very much in
> love with each other and wanted very much
> to see each other. One slight complication:
> no boat, and an alligator-filled river stood
> between them.

> Abigail decided to seek help so that she could
> see her boyfriend, Greg. She approached
> Sinbad the Sailor and asked if she could bor-
> row his boat. Sinbad thought for a moment
> and then replied: "Sure, you can borrow my
> boat, but only under one condition. The con-
> dition is that you sleep with me tonight."
> Now, this startled Abigail, because she didn't
> want to sleep with Sinbad—she just wanted to
> borrow his boat so she could see Greg.

After Abigail had told Sinbad "no deal," she wandered down the road until she came upon Ivan the Uninvolved. Abigail explained her plight (her desire to see Greg, Sinbad's response) to Ivan, who, as his name indicates, didn't give a darn. Ivan told Abigail: "Hey, don't bother me. That's not my concern. I don't care what happens. Take off." A despondent Abigail, her options exhausted, finally decided to go back to Sinbad. She slept with him that night. The next morning, Sinbad, true to his word, loaned his boat to Abigail. Abigail sailed across the river and saw her beloved Greg. After spending a few delightful hours together, Abigail felt compelled to tell Greg what had happened. After she had related her whole story, Greg completely blew up. "You what? I can't believe you did that. I—I can't believe you slept with him! That's it—it's all over—just forget the relationship—get out of my life!"

Distraught, Abigail wandered off. She came upon Stan the Schlemiel. Borrowing his shoulder to shed her tears, Abigail related her tale to Stan. Stan then went looking for Greg (with Abigail close behind). Stan found Greg and proceeded to beat the stuffing out of him, while Abigail gleefully and laughingly applauding the bloody pummeling.[2]

After the reading, the participants were instructed on how to teach the lesson to their students. Each student was to rank in order the characters from most to least despicable, gather in small groups, and come to a consensus of rank order. To do this, each student must follow the seven steps of the Values Clarification.

The Seven Steps of Values Clarification

1. Choose freely his own values.

2. Seek alternatives when making value choices.

3. Feel good about his choices and values.

4. Be aware of consequences of his choices.

5. Be willing to affirm his choices publicly.

6. Act on his choice.

7. Act on his choices repeatedly as to form a pattern in life.[3]

From this exercise, the students learned that they have control over their lives and that whatever "value" decision they made was right for them. But is it? Is it morally or ethically right to have "sex" before marriage or to compromise your belief system to get what you want? Is it morally or ethically right to willfully get back at someone who hurt you? Suppose Abigail had "felt good" about killing Greg. Would "feeling good" about your choice make it right? Is values clarification saying to children that whatever you choose to value will be right for you, because you chose it? Yes, I believe that is what it means.

Abigail chose to sleep with Sinbad so she could see her beloved Greg. According to the "Value" experts, this is okay because she chose freely and acted upon her choice. In values clarification, there is no right and wrong answer; everything is relative, personal, and situational. You decide what is right for you and act upon it. Sounds scary, doesn't it? I wonder if this is the reason that 60 percent of children have self-gratification as their main purpose in life and why 21 percent of elementary children would try to cheat on tests and, finally, that 65 percent of high-schoolers say they would cheat in order to get ahead?[4]

Where is the moral teaching? Thirty years ago, schools could teach that it was wrong to lie or steal, but not today. Today, teachers cannot say what is right or wrong because that would indicate to some child that their decision was not the right "choice." Teachers can't moralize. Dr. Robert Coles, a psychiatrist, expressed his shock at this.

"Once, teachers were invested with moral authority. Religion was taught in schools, and children prayed at the beginning and end of the day. Children stood and saluted the flag . . . when religion was removed from the schools, secular humanism came along to take its place, and teachers were stripped of the moral authority they once had. In effect, we have removed right and wrong from schools. And when you do that, you remove discipline. How can you have discipline when nothing is wrong?"[5]

If the moral law is not an objective reality, then no choice can be better than another choice. Today, according to the "value experts," whatever moral decision a child makes will be right for him, because he chose it.

Social Studies

Teachers use a variety of methods and activities to teach values clarification to students. One method might be to incorporate the values into the subject matter, such as a social studies lesson on values statements:

"Any act of violence is wrong." "It is better to have inflation and no unemployment, than no inflation and some unemployment." "Congress should allocate more funds for programs to eliminate poverty."[6]

These statements represent the new insurgence of value statements being put into the social studies curriculum on a daily basis. How do students in social studies class feel about value statements? Most students have said: "... Your opinion is as good as mine," or "How could you believe something so out of line with the values of your parents, friends, and leaders of this country?"[7]

But, educators feel that students need to become critical thinkers and not always agree on what parents or other authority figures feel on an issue. The emphasis of the social studies curriculum is not content, but problems, issues, controversy, and the decision-making process. The new curriculum focuses on students making value judgments and policy decisions. It is no longer a teacher-centered classroom, but one that zeros in on attacking issues and coming up with alternative solutions. Value questioning and inquiry methods are two areas parents need to watch closely.

When parents think that their child will be learning "how a bill becomes a law" or "supply and demand," they had better do their homework to see if the concept is being taught or if the child is learning a new value system.

To keep an eye on what is happening in your child's class, have him carry an assignment notebook and request that assignments be written down and signed by the teacher. Most schools employ this tool, and it will help you to know what questions to ask him about the class.

Classroom Strategies

Listed below are sixteen commonly used strategies for teaching values clarification in the public schools. Many of the strategies include role-playing, diary writing, checklists, group discussion, and problem solving. Each strategy will be defined and analyzed.

1. Value Love List

In a large room with moveable chairs, a small group of participants is asked to order activities they love to do. The teacher then helps direct the students to what he values by asking them to:

• Place a "$" sign by the activity that cost three or more dollars;

• Place a "10" next to the activity you would not have done ten years ago;

• Place an "X" by the activity you want people to know that you do;

• Place an "M" by the activity you did this month;

• Place a "T" by the activity that takes you ten hours a day to complete;

• Place an "E" by the activity you read, think, worry, or plan about;

• Place a "C" by the activity that you feel made you grow.[8]

From this list, the teacher can help the student realize where his values lie. Students compare first and second rankings and end in small groups sharing what they learned.

Discovering your values doesn't seem all bad if you are talking about honesty or loyalty. But what happens when you get into areas that conflict with moral, biblical principles? How is a second grader going to handle criticism from the teacher or group when he admits that what he values most is going to Sunday school?

Since the goals of this activity can be to introduce students to values clarification, define a value, or discern values from value indicators, this type of activity can be found in any class. When your child talks about how he orders his own personal values, your alarm bells should ring. This is where an assignment notebook to keep track of what he is doing in that class will help you.

2. Value Auction

A forty-five minute activity for twelve participants and one auctioneer, which focuses on:

1. What life value is of most importance;
2. Developing trust;
3. Analyzing competition and cooperation.[9]

This is a smorgasbord of buying and selling values. Students determine their most important life values and how these affect their lives.

3. Value Voting

Students divide into two groups. Representatives from each group are chosen to analyze the value, while the other members listen. One group is for the value and the other against it. As a group, they complete the basic values steps:

• publicly affirm their stand on the issue;
• look at alternative values;
• explore value concerns of other students;
• explore the value issues of the group;

A technique used in values voting is "Psychic Power Discovery." The title indicates that students use their "psychic powers" to know a person's deepest thoughts.[10]

4. Value Ranking

Value ranking can be a group activity in which a teacher reads the values, and students rank order them. Or, it can be a "sub-group" activity in which students order values, without any teacher direction. In listing one value per column, students learn what value is most important to them. The main goals point to consequences. The students must, in all cases, look at the consequences of their chosen values or alternative values. This can make the child question his value choice and put him in a position of being publicly ridiculed by his peers for his personal decision. Instead of allowing him to openly say, "This is what I believe," the child must take that value, consider all the issues of today and see if that value is true[11]— a tough decision for a ten-year-old.

5. Value Continuum

This is group activity that encourages breaking down opinions on an issue before that issue becomes polarized. An example would be a value continuum dealing with the homosexual movement, where the pro-gay and anti-gay positions are argued. Both sides must agree on possible variables within an issue and consider all possible alternatives before coming to a conclusion. One outcome that no one can take is an extreme view. Since each student has to say where he would be on the continuum, the chance for compromising his or her convictions could occur because of peer pressure.[12]

6. Incomplete Value Questions

As a parent, how would you respond if you knew the teacher confronted your child about the real reason he values something, or questions your child's beliefs in front of the class. This activity does just that! It forces students to question their values and explores why they believe them. The activity opens the door to students questioning whether they chose their values freely. This is an example of the open ended statement technique, in which any number of students are used to complete the exercise.[13]

7. Coat of Arms

This is a values clarification activity used to help students discover and publicly affirm their values. Students are told the coat of arms was a symbol for family values and now they can fantasize and discover their own values. Would you think your family values are being attacked if these questions were asked of your child?

1. Is there something that keeps you from enjoying your family?

2. What is the most uncomfortable time you have had with your family?

3. What is the common thread in your family?

4. What is something you do with your family?

5. What fun have you had with your family in the last ___ months?

6. What changes would you like in your family?

7. What does the family do best together? [14]

8. Value Thought Sheet

Students are to choose an event or thought that has occurred or happened to them in the past week. After the students have shared the information in a subgroup, the teacher explains the methods for discovering values and value indicators. Students publicly affirm the chosen value before the group and the activity ends with the student exploring all aspects of their chosen value. The goals of the activity are:

1. to discover events and the values emerging from them;

2. to look to others for advice on other alternatives and consequences of these events;

3. for students to work together to choose value topics;

4. to share thoughts about their values;

To facilitate discussion and involvement, the teacher may direct students to some questions.

1. Is the value a cherished belief?

2. Do you accept your value?

3. Does the thought sheet reflect your life goal?

4. Does the thought sheet point to possible problems?[15]

9. Value Autobiography

In a small group, students share their personal history through developing various graphs that include family life, hobbies, friends, beliefs, reading, etc. Students are directed to answer questions about their lives. They also form subgroups to discover their values and analyze their choices.[16]

This is activity where students learn to question what they believe.

10. Value-Clarification Journal

This is a daily journal that shows how the student has developed and used his values in his daily life. Students record class events that helped them to choose, prize, or act on their value. Emphasis is placed on the "process" of one's value development. What follows are open-ended statements the teacher may pose to probe student thinking:

1. I have learned that I . . .
2. I realize that I . . .
3. I never knew that I . . .
4. I know now that I . . .
5. I have discovered that I . . .
6. I have relearned that I . . .[17]

11. Value Questions

The purpose of this exercise is to show students the:

1. definition of a value;
2. how to use the "8" criteria for discovering their values;
3. compare values with indicators.[18]

Students work together to order their values and compare them with the eight basic value question worksheets. If they agree it is not a true value, students work to change it by using the eight questions.

Describe the value:

1. Have I freely chosen this value?
2. From among what alternatives? (List)
3. What are the consequences of choosing this value?
4. How recently have I acted on this value?

5. In what way has this value become a regular pattern in my life?

6. When did I most recently/publicly affirm this value? (Give details)

7. How do I prize or celebrate this value in my life?

8. How does this value help me to grow as a person?[19]

12. Value Interview

Here, a student must defend his values with the interviewer and the group. After completing this activity, students should understand one anothers' values, how they came to choose those values, and should discover new options for people with different values. When it is clear that a particular value is not accepted, students may divide into two groups and try to reach a compromise.[20]

13. Value Brainstorming

Students brainstorm ideas to a teacher who records and ranks their values. After students have exhausted their ideas, they form groups to order and prize their values. The goal is for students to explore value-laden words, attitudes in values, and to learn to negotiate their values.[21] This is an activity that takes place in many classrooms across the country.

14. Polarizing Positions

The object of this lesson is to learn from different people who don't agree and to show alternatives to choosing the value. A student goes before the group, explains his value and how he arrived at it. The student body then questions him about the validity of the value, how he arrived at it, how he prizes it, and how he has acted on it.[22] Another activity places the student on the "hotseat" for his beliefs.

15. Life Raft

This is an activity that plays on the feelings and emotions of students. The students are instructed to sit on the floor and pretend that they are in a "life raft." The scene is set by asking the participants to imagine that they have been on an Atlantic cruise, that a serious storm has developed, that their ship has been struck by lightning, and that they have all had to get into a life raft. The teacher explains that the major problem that now exists is that the raft has room and food enough for only nine persons and there are ten in the group. One person must be sacrificed in order to save the rest. The facilitator informs the group that the decision is to be made by a group consensus. Each member is to "plead his case" to the others, arguing why he should live, and then the group is to decide who must go overboard. He tells the participants that they have one-half hour to make their decision. At the end of that time, the life raft will sink if there are still ten people in it. He puts a manual alarm clock near the participants so that they can hear it tick and sets the alarm to go off in one-half hour.[23]

Students are to reflect on what values are in the situation and ask the following questions:

1. What kind of value assumptions did members of the group make?

2. What values were the members acting on?

3. What did you learn about your values from an experiential standpoint?

4. In light of this experience, how do you value your own life and the lives of others?

5. What is your worth?[24]

16. Value Role Play

In a role playing situation, students explore the values of two or more people and how these values can cause conflict.

The teacher describes a role for each student. The role might be:

Father: You love your kids and you want to send them to college, but you feel unappreciated because they do not seem to be interested in going to college.

Mother: You love your family and agree with your husband that the kids should go to college. You cannot understand why they do not seem to appreciate his desire to give them a better education.

Son: You are seventeen-years-old, a senior in high school, and you do not want to go to college. You are not sure what you want to do, but you like to work with your hands and think you would like to become an electrician, machinist, or carpenter.

Daughter: You are sixteen-years-old, a junior in high school, and do not want to go to college. You would just like to be married, but do not know what to do in the meantime.[25]

The teacher keeps the focus of the students on discovering their values, feelings, and attitudes and then points the group toward processing the information and developing a better understanding of different values.

Perhaps this section on the sixteen most commonly used value strategies will help parents to focus on what to look for in their children's assignments, curriculum, and supplemental materials. Today, more than ever, children need the parental instruction on how to counter these strategies and to understand and apply their beliefs.

Classroom Activities

Knowing the sixteen basic strategies used to teach values to children is vital if parents are to combat this movement. Equally important are various popular classroom activities that are used in classrooms to promote and incorporate values clarification. These activities can be found in any curriculum: social studies, language arts, math, science, health, etc.

New Planet

An activity frequently used in a social studies classes is defining a "New Planet." Students gather in small groups. The teacher distributes lists of suggestions from which the students must collectively make decisions regarding their new planet. According to the teacher directions, all the students must agree to questions in the book *Developing Individual Values in the Classroom*, in which Richard and Geri Curwin give step-by-step directions for the activity:

1. Will there be population control or no population control?

If you choose population control, the planet will never be over-populated and conditions will be much more pleasant. There will be more for everyone, and life will be more enjoyable. However, the government will determine who can have children and how many they may have. There will be stiff penalties for the birth of unlicensed children. If you choose to have no population control, the government will have no say. There might, however, be over-population and all the problems that go with it.

2. Will there be naturally grown food, or will it be created by chemical and artificial means?

If the food is grown naturally, it will be healthy and tasty. There will be less chance of diseases that result from chemical and artificial processing. But, there will be less food produced, and everyone will have to eat less. If food is produced artificially, there will be more than enough for all; however, it will taste rather bland and uninteresting. It will also not be as healthy for people as organic food.

3. Will the government be run by a single authority, such as a king or dictator, or will it be a democracy run by and for the people?

If the society is run by one individual, he will be the wisest and best able to deal with problems because of his great skill in governing. He will have the best staff possible to aid in his decision. He will have absolute power to make the rules. If the government is determined by popular vote, no one individual will have absolute power. All decisions will be decided by popular vote. The best decisions might not be made, but all individuals in society will have an equal voice.

4. Will there be industrialism or no industrialism?

If there is industrialism, there will be many consumer goods for all. The land will be torn up for raw materials and there will be pollution problems. There might be an energy crisis eventually as fuels are expended. If there is no industrialism, there will be no mass-produced materials and everything will be made by hand. It will take longer to accomplish nearly everything, but the land will remain beautiful, and there will be no shortage of energy. Pollution will not be a problem.

5. Will there be advanced methods of transportation, or will the different communities be isolated?

With transportation systems, there will be potential fuel crisis and a possible pollution problem. The natural landscape will be torn up for roads, parking lots, airports, train tracks and stations. Noise will also be a problem. If there is no structured transportation system, each colony will be isolated from others. People will have trouble getting to stores and hospitals. It will be difficult for people in different colonies to visit one another.

6. Will there be a uniform culture or many subcultures?

If there is a uniform culture, everyone will be alike. There will be no diversity and no threat from groups who want to change things. There will be no bigotry, and society will run smoothly. If there are different cultures, there will be diversity, and each culture will be able to learn from the other cultures. There will be the possibility of change—life will be dynamic. There will also be a chance for prejudice and conflict to arise in the different cultures.

7. *Will formal education be compulsory, or will each child and family have free choice about going to school?*

If school is mandatory, all children will have to go to a state-controlled or -approved school. There will be no exceptions. Everyone will receive the same education. If there is free choice in education, then each family will be able to decide on what kind of education their children will receive. The quality of education will be uneven.

8. *Will there be equal supplies and materials for all, or will some get more while others get less?*

If everyone gets the same amount, no one will go hungry or be in need. Those who work the hardest will earn the same amount as those who don't work at all. If each person gets only what he earns, there will be inequities in the amount of goods that a person gets. There might be poor people who go hungry, while the rich may have more than they can use.

9. *Will there be guns for everyone or for no one?*

If everyone has a gun, each person will have an equal chance in times of danger. Hunting will be easier, and sport shooting will be allowed. If no one has a gun, no one will be shot. Hunting will be more difficult, and there will be no sport shooting.

10. *Will there be government files on every individual or no files on anyone at all?*

If there are files on individuals, it will be easy to keep track of criminals and those who don't pay their debts. Any time a government official wants or needs to find information on a citizen, he will be able to just check the file and find out what he wants to know. Employers and other people will be able to get file information if the government believes there is good reason. If there are no files, it will be more difficult for the government in keeping track of the deviant elements of society; but under this system, every citizen will have his privacy, and no one's rights will be abused.[26]

After the students have read the questions, they are to discuss them and come to a conclusion on how these statements affect them and their society.

If this is not an anti-American, anti-family, anti-God activity, I don't know what is. The "New Planet" activity is nothing more than a New Age philosophy being shoved into our children's minds through mind games and manipulation. What child doesn't want a perfect environment, good health and easy living? According to this activity a master king and his officials will take care of you. You won't experience crime because there will be no guns. In addition, the file they keep on you will tell them everything they want to know about you at any given time. Now if students are receiving this message as good and fair, over time they may believe it. This doesn't sound like a social studies lesson that I learned twenty years ago in school. Maybe this is the reason for the decrease in patriotism, free-enterprise, and family values in American society today.

Value Folders

Another classroom activity that should send the alarm bells ringing is "Value Folders." This activity is for seventh and eighth grade students. Students select pictures from magazines, paste them in a folder and include two or more questions about each picture.

An example:

    (picture of children)

    Do these children feel more or less successful than others? Why do you think so?

    (picture of school)

    How do you feel about school?

    (picture of a group of people)

    What is friendship?

    Of what value is it to know others well?[27]

This activity focuses on students formulating their values through group discussion. All student responses are kept in the "value folder." It's a unique way for teachers to keep track of how students are processing in their "new" values; at the end of the school year, the folders are given to the next teacher.

Parents need to ask teachers if they keep the value folders, sheets, or anything that lists their child's values. If they do, where do they store them? What happens to them? Who gets to see them? How are they used?

Ask to see you child's cumulative file. Read all the information over carefully to see if there is any reference to what your child believes. Look carefully at psychological or counselor evaluations. Teachers who sit in on review meetings can give a written report, which can include this type of information. From this information, they can suggest individual or peer counseling. What started out as an innocent activity could prove deadly to a child who has been taught at home to believe in absolutes.

My House

Another popular activity is "My House." In this activity, children draw their house and the people who live there. Then they are asked to write a story about how their family communicates. Experts feel this is a good jumping-off point for discussing how families live together.[28]

Why does anyone need to know how your family communicates? Is this infringing on family privacy rights? Maybe this is the reason your child doesn't communicate well with you, or disagrees with you. Is he learning techniques to counter what you are saying?

The Authority Figure

The "Authority Figure" activity has students writing answers to various questions:

1. If you were to choose one adult, either real-life or fiction, to be in direct control of your life for the next year, who would it be?

2. What are three things about this person that you admire?

3. What are three things about this person you dislike?

4. If you chose a real person, when was the last time that you sat down and talked with this person for more than half an hour?

5. Is this person like you in any way?[29]

Student responses will be shared with other classmates. The object of the lesson is for students to learn about themselves. But is it? The teachers' manual tells the instructor to probe deep into the child's private thoughts to learn how the child thinks and believes. Why does a teacher need to know your child's deepest thoughts? his deepest beliefs?

Responding to God

This activity "What I Might Tell My Older Brother or Sister?" poses this question to students: "I got mad at God. What should I do?"[30]

Do you want a person who believes in "value clarifying" telling your child how to respond to God? When we can't even whisper God's name or the Bible in schools, they can tell your child how to respond to Him?

This is an activity that could lead to the counselors' office. Children trust counselors. They might confide in him and seek help on how to respond to the teachers' suggestions. Hopefully, the counselor will direct your child to seek help from you, but don't count on it.

Student Obituaries

Another activity that usually sends a child to the counselors' office is "Funeral Notice," a morbid activity that forces children to face their mortality. Students read and discuss obituaries. The class activity is to write their own obituaries from the following questions:

1. What would you want others to read in the paper about your life?

2. What are some things of importance about you that others should know?

3. How long do you want to live?

4. Do you think that length of life or quality of life is more important?

5. Do you measure the worth of a person by

his character or by what he has? (Good looks, money, position, etc.).[31]

Here are some examples of student obituaries:

> Yesterday, March 30, 2012, the deceased passed away, 55 years after her birth. A Straight "A" student through most of her life, the deceased was the 1976 Miss America winner. In her winning speech, she stressed the importance of a good education, and went on to state that nothing is more important in a person's life than the love and guidance one receives from family and friends.
>
> The deceased and her best friend Maggie Grady shared a double wedding in the year 1980, at the age of 23. She spent her honeymoon as a guest at the 22nd Olympiad. She was the owner of the "cleanest spot in America," Sugar Pine, California. She bought this lumber camp and kept all factories, cars and other such polluters out of the environment. She left Sugar Pine to her four daughters, Rachel, Julie, Rhonda and Sheryl, to be turned into one of the few true nature exhibits left in America.
>
> She died of natural causes, and her last request was that her body was to be donated to science for the betterment of mankind. Memorial services will be held in the home of her parents.
>
> ✍ ✍ ✍ ✍
>
> ....Died in the hospital yesterday from wounds received in a gun battle with a sniper. He was hit in the right leg while getting from his car to investigate a beating. He was hit

again in the chest while getting behind the
car and was unconscious when help arrived.
He was 38, a 17 year veteran of the police
force. He is survived by his wife Julie, a daughter Ann, and two sons, Jason and Brian. Services are to be held tomorrow at St. Mary's
Catholic Church.

    ✍   ✍   ✍   ✍

. . . .The victim died on December 30, 1977 at
12:30 P.M. Her body was found in her one-
room apartment in the Hollywood Hills. Her
death was caused from an overdose of sleep-
ing pills. Police said it was accidental suicide.
She was twenty years old and was attending
U.C.L.A. here in Los Angeles. She was to
graduate and get her degree to become a
medical social worker. She also had a part-
time modeling job with an agency in Hollywood. She had many friends and loved helping people. Her goal in life was to be successful. She is survived by her parents, one brother
and her fiance.

    ✍   ✍   ✍   ✍

. . . .Being an adventurous girl, she didn't want
to be told how things worked or why, but
experienced them herself, and sought the answers. She seemed so full of life and often
said how happy she was to be alive, but believ-
ing that death can strike anytime, she always
got the most from life that she could, and, in
turn, offered her love to anyone who needed
or wanted it. She believed that happiness was
achieved through life.[32]

Questioning Technique

In middle school or high-school, students can be presented with a provocative quotation, such as: . . . .Gustave O. Faubert said, "Nothing great is done without fanaticism. Fanaticism is religion, and the eighteenth century 'philosophers' who decreed the former actually overthrew the latter. Fanaticism is faith, the essence of faith, burning faith, active faith, the faith that works miracles. . ."[33]

When all the students demonstrate understanding of the quote, they are asked to answer the questions.

1. Are you a fanatic about anything?

2. What groups of people in our society seem fanatical to you? Why would you or wouldn't you join them in their efforts? What is better about your alternative?

3. How did you arrive at your decision about what to do?

4. Have you done anything lately about what you believe?[34]

Patriotism

Depicting religion as fanaticism is one approach to demeaning traditional values. Another less obvious approach is attacking the character of past leaders. For instance:

His duplicity sinks deeper and deeper into my mind. His hatred of Hamilton was unbounded; of John Marshall, most intense; of my father, tempered with compunctious visitings, always controlled by his ambition...he died insolvent, and on the very day of his death received eleemosynary donations from

the charity of some of those whom he had
most deeply injured.[35]

Assassinating the character of our past leaders is one way to discourage patriotism and move
in the direction of general acceptance of a one
world government, an agenda item of the "New
Age."

Honesty

Do you remember the old golden rule you
learned in school—honesty is always the best policy?
Today, students can't always apply this rule, because when they are taught honesty, they have
value "choices." Adults must not impart their values on others; so, there may be times, they are
told, that you can be dishonest; it depends on
your choices. Here is an example of a class activity
teaching "honesty":

> *Teacher:* So, some of you think it is best to be
> honest on tests, is that right? (Some heads
> nod affirmatively.) And, some of you think
> dishonesty is all right? (A few hesitant and
> slight nods.) And, I guess some of you are not
> certain. (Heads nod.) Well, are there any
> choices, or is it just a matter of dishonesty
> versus honesty?

> *Sam:* You could be honest some of the time
> and dishonest some of the time.

> *Teacher:* Does that sound like a possible
> choice, class? (Heads nod) Any other alter-
> natives to choose from?

> *Tracy:* You could be honest in some situa-
> tions and not in others. For example, I am
> not honest when a friend asks about an ugly
> dress, at least sometimes. (Laughter)

Teacher: Is that a possible choice, class? (Heads nod again.) Any other alternatives?

Sam: It seems to me that you have to be all one way or all the other.

Teacher: Just a minute, Sam. As usual, we are first looking for the alternatives that there are in the issue. Later, we'll try to look at the consequences of the alternatives we've identified. Any other alternatives, class? (No response.) Well, then let's list the four possibilities that we have on the board and I'm going to ask that each of you do two things for yourself: (1) see if you can identify any other choices in this issue of honesty and dishonesty, and (2) consider the consequences of each alternative and see which ones you prefer. Later, we will have buzz groups in which you can discuss this to see if you are able to get clear about this.

Ginger: Does that mean we can decide for ourselves whether we should be honest on tests here?

Teacher: No, that means that you can decide on the value. I personally value honesty, and although you may choose to be dishonest, I shall insist that we be honest on our tests here. In other areas of your life, you may have more freedom to be dishonest, but one can't do anything any time. In this class, I shall expect honesty on tests.

Ginger: But, then how can we decide for ourselves? Aren't you telling us what to value?

Sam: Sure, you're telling us what we should do and believe in.

Teacher: Not exactly. I don't mean to tell you what you should value. That's up to you. But,

I do mean that in this class, not necessarily elsewhere, you have to be honest on tests or suffer certain consequences. I merely mean that I cannot give tests without the rule of honesty. All of you who choose dishonesty as a value may not practice it here, that's all I'm saying.[36]

In this activity, teachers feel that students are making clear choices for their own value world. And, it doesn't matter if their choices are dishonest

Meditation Room

Students are to read "The Meditation Room at the U.N." and answer the questions. It's non-graded activity that students will discuss in class. Here is an example of the reading, which includes a quote from Miss Mannes:

There is a chapel, or meditation room, at the U.N. General Assembly building in New York that has had all symbols of particular religions removed. There is nothing there but some rows of chairs, and a potted plant. "It seemed to me, standing there, that this nothingness was so oppressive and disturbing that it became a sort of madness, and the room a sort of padded cell. It seemed to me that the core of our greatest contemporary trouble lay here—that all this whiteness and shapelessness and weakness was the leukemia of non-commitment, sapping our strength. We had found, finally, that only nothing could please all, and we were trying to make the greatest of all generalities out of that most singular truth, the spirit of man. The terrifying thing about this room was that it made no state-

ment whatever. In its capacity and construction, it could not even act as a reflector of
thought.[37]

Students are to answer the following question:

1. Write your reaction to this quotation in
just a few words.

2. Does it produce a strong emotion in you?
What emotion does it produce?

3. Do you think Miss Mannes' quotation is
"anti-religious"? If no, why? If yes, in which ways?

4. In your mind, does Miss Mannes, in the
quotation above, exaggerate the danger which she
sees? Explain.

5. Can you list some more examples in our
society which tend to support Miss Mannes' point?

6. Can you list any which tend to refute her
point of view?

7. If this quotation suggests a problem which
worries you, are there some things you might personally do about it? within yourself? with some
close friends? with the larger society?

8. Is there any wisdom from the past which
you can cite to ease Miss Mannes' concern? Is
there any wisdom from the past which might alarm
her even more?

9. What do you get aroused about? Are you
doing anything about it?[38]

This may be a non-graded and an optional
assignment, but it still takes place more often then
you think. It's another exercise where your child
has to defend his faith. And, his responses go on
record and are placed in his "values folder."

Autobiographical Questionnaire

The last activity I want to share with you is an example of an "Autobiographical Questionnaire." I believe this activity carries a lot of weight for four reasons: (1) It gives a complete family history; (2) It is kept in the child's value folder; (3) It's used as a reference for teaching the child; (4) It can be passed on to the next teacher. Listed below is a sample Autobiographical Questionnaire that is used in classrooms today:

1. *Name*_____

2. *Birthday* _____*Age in Years*_____
3. *Address*_____

4. *What other schools did you go to? Tell me something about them.*

5. *Who are the people in your family? If you had to use two sentences to describe each person, what would you say about each member of your family?*
_____

6. *Have you any ideas about what you would like to do when you grow up?* _____

7. *What possibilities have you talked over with your parents?* _____

8. *What does your father do for a living?* _____

9. *What are some of his interests, hobbies, etc.? What does he do when he isn't working?* _____

10. *Does your mother work?* _____

11. *What are her interests, hobbies, etc?* _____

12. *How do you spend your time after school?* ___

13. *Of all the things you do in your free time, which do you like most?* _____

14. *Which do you like least?* _____

15. *What does your family usually do for Thanks-giving? Christmas?* _____

16. *What have you done the last two summers?* __

17. *What have you done the last two Christmas vacations?* _____

18. *What magazines do you read regularly?* _____

19. *Do you subscribe to any yourself?* _____

20. *What are your favorite TV shows?* _____

21. *Have you seen any movies in the past few months which you particularly liked?* _____

22. *Tell me a sentence or two about each movie, and why you liked it.* _____

23. *What are your favorite sports, if any?* _____

24. *If I were to ask you what books you've read and which you've liked the best, what would you answer?* _____

25. *Do you work after school or on Saturdays? Where? What are you using the money for?* ____

26. *What do you like best about school?* _____

27. *What do you like least about school?* _____

28. *If you could change some part of your educational program, what would it be?* _____

29. *If you were a teacher, how would you teach your classes?* _____

30. *Have you a hobby that requires much of your time? What is it?* _____

31. *How did you get interested in it?* _____

32. *Which of your friends are interested in it with you?* _____

33. Who are some of your friends who aren't interested in this activity?

*34. Is there an adult outside of school whom you dislike intensely? Why?*_____

35. Are there some adults outside of school whom you admire intensely? Why? _____

*36. Do you have some good ideas about things which you might like to mention?*_____

*37. Have you ever invented anything? What?*_____

*38. What is there about you which makes your friends like you?*_____

*39. Is there something you want badly, but can't quite afford right now? What?*_____

*40. Of all the people you know who have helped you, who has helped the most? How did they go about it?[39]*_____

This activity goes beyond the information stage. It probes deep into the family structure and gleans information that is normally non-accessible. Why does anyone need to know your parents' hobbies, or where you spent the last two Christmas'? Is this valid information that will help instruct your child?

Ask your child's teacher if an "Autobiographical Questionnaire" has been filled out. If he has, ask the teacher what he or she is going to use it for and where is it being filed? If you do not get a clear answer, check your child's cumulative folder and values folder and make a copy of it for your personal use.

Parent Response

When your child brings home his assignments, check whether any of the following symbols are on it (Symbols used for grading student papers are found in *Values and Teaching, Second Edition*, written by Merrill Hermin, Howard Kirschnbaum, and Sidney B. Simon.):

> E—Extremes (all, non-, every, never, always, etc.) Questions for teachers to ask: "Are you sure? Would you change this on reconsideration?"
>
> I—Indefinites (some, seldom, sometimes, perhaps, a few, might, etc.) "Is this unnecessarily vague? Can you be more specific?"
>
> VJ—Value Judgments (wasted time, a good lesson, it was unfortunate, a difficult job, a wonderful man, etc.) "Are you making a judgment that others might not agree with? Do you want to be more objective here?"
>
> AT—Attributing a situation or a person's feelings to unstated evidence (she overlooked the student; he wanted to cry; she felt badly; he teased her; Sal likes reading; they were afraid to answer; a productive lesson, etc.) "Are you sure? Have you made it clear to the reader that this is only your inference from the data? Would it be better to omit this, or state the basis for our interpretation?"
>
> ALT—Alternatives (either we do this or that; if this happens, then that results; John should do thus-and-so; from the information, we can conclude such-and-such; etc.) "Are there other alternatives? Have you considered other possibilities?"
>
> GN—Generalizations (since our friends like

it, boys everywhere will; after examining three towns. . . ; an authority states. . . ; after talking to him for five minutes, I could tell what kind of person he was; etc.) "Have you over generalized? Do you have enough data for the conclusion you are making?"

OS—Over-simplification (money leads to happiness; a college education will make a cultured man; Japan started the war; we need more scientists to win the cold war; etc.) "Have you oversimplified the situation? Have you inappropriately reduced a complex situation to simple terms?"

PR—Projection (teachers deserve higher salaries; he should quit; they discriminate against people like me; bright students; should get more attention than dull students; John cannot be taught anything; etc.) "Have you examined your own motives here? Could it be that you are projecting your own feelings into the situation, perhaps not consciously?"

D—Dogmatic "Are you sure? Have you considered alternatives"[40]

Knowing these symbols will enable you to determine if your child is receiving values clarification materials.

After you have gone over the values clarification assignments, teachers ask your child the following questions (These are the "thirty clarifying responses" teachers use with students to probe their belief systems.):

Thirty Clarifying Responses

1. Is this something that you prize?

2. Are you glad about that?

3. How did you feel when that happened?

4. Did you consider any alternatives?

5. Have you felt this way for a long time?

6. Was that something that you, yourself, selected or chose?

7. Did you have to choose that? was it a free choice?

8. Do you do anything about the idea?

9. Can you give me some examples of that idea?

10. What do you mean by _____? can you define that word?

11. Where would that idea lead? what would be its consequences?

12. Would you really do that, or are you just talking?

13. Are you saying that . . . (repeat statement to student in some distorted way)?

14. Did you say that . . . (repeat statement to student in some distorted way)?

15. Have you thought much about that idea (or behavior)?

16. What are some good things about that notion?

17. What do we have to assume for things to work out that way?

18. Is what you express consistent with . . . (Note something else the person said or did that may point to an inconsistency.)?

19. What other possibilities are there?

20. Is that a personal preference, or do you think most people should believe that?

21. How can I help you do something about your idea?

22. Is there a purpose behind this activity?

23. Is that very important to you?

24. Do you do this often?

25. Would you like to tell others about your idea?

26. Do you have any reasons for saying (or doing) that?

27. Would you do the same thing over again?

28. How do you know it's right?

29. Do you value that?

30. Do you think people will always believe that?[41]

Knowing how the assignments are graded and what questions are being asked of your child about the assignments will help you in combatting this intrusion. Another helpful piece of information to remember is that when teachers are teaching a values clarification assignment, to be effective they must:

  • be accepting and non-judgmental;

  • encourage diversity; realize that there are no absolute right or wrong answers for anyone's values questions;

• respect the individual's choice to partici-
pate or not;

• respect the individual's response;

• encourage each person to answer honestly;

• listen and raise clarifying questions with the
students;

• avoid questions which might threaten or
limit thinking;

• raise questions of both personal and social
concern.[42]

Being able to understand how values clarification works in the schools will enable you to
detect how the New Age agenda gets through the
school doors and into the classroom.

The Kohlberg Theory

For years American schools indirectly taught
that one should work hard, study diligently, and
respect his parents, teachers and authority. Parents and churches instilled the values of honesty,
and right and wrong. But, today, these values have
been replaced by a new theory: that there is no
right and wrong, and that it is not enlightened to
believe in a moral authority.

Lawrence Kohlberg, a professor at Harvard
University, developed a theory of moral thought
that is used in our public schools and other moral
development programs across the country. His
theory leaves out God and any reference to religious beliefs. In *Moral Education: The Role of the
School*, Donald Peckenpaugh describes Kohlberg's
six stages to ethical awareness.

At stage one, good and bad are defined in
terms of avoidance of punishment and deference
to power. At stage two, right consists of that which

satisfies one's own needs and occasionally the needs of others. At stage three, good behavior is that which pleases others and is approved by them. At stage four, right behavior consists of doing one's duty and maintaining the social order. At stage five, right action tends to be defined in terms of general rights and standards that have been critically examined and agreed upon by the whole society. At stage six, right is defined by the decision of conscience in accord with self-chosen ethical principles appealing to logical comprehensiveness.[43]

The following chart gives a clear picture of the "Kohlberg" theory:

Table 1
The Six Stages of Moral Judgment *

(Content of Stage: What is Right and Reasons for Doing Right)

Level and Stage:
Level 1: Preconventional
Stage 1: Heteronomous morality

What is Right: Sticking to rules backed by punishment; obedience for its own sake; avoiding physical damage to persons and property.

Reasons for Doing Right: Avoidance of punishment, superior power of authorities.

Social Perspective of Stage: Egocentric point of view. Doesn't consider the interests of others or recognize that they differ; doesn't relate

___
* Source: Lawrence Kohlberg, *"Moral Stage and Moralization: The Cognitive-Developmental Approach, in Moral Development and Behavior: Theory, Research and Social Issues,* ed. Thomas Lickona (New York: Holt, Rhinehart and Winston, 1976), pp. 34-35.

two points of view. Actions considered physically, rather than in terms of psychological interests of others. Confusion of authority's perspective with one's own.

Level and Stage:
Level I:
Stage 2: Individualism, instrumental purpose, and exchange.

What is Right: Following rules only when in one's immediate interest; acting to meet one's needs or interests in a world where one has to recognize that other people also have interests.

Reasons for Doing Right: To serve one's own needs or interests in a world where one has to recognize that other people also have interests.

Social Perspective of Stage: Concrete individualistic perspective. Aware that everybody has interests to pursue and that these can conflict: right is relative (in the concrete individualistic sense).

Level and Stage:
Level II: Conventional.
Stage 3: Mutual interpersonal expectations, relationships, and interpersonal conformity.

What is Right: Living up to what is expected by people close to you or what people generally expect of a son, brother, friend, etc. "Being good" is important and means having good motives, showing concern for others. It also means keeping mutual relationships such as trust, loyalty, respect, and gratitude.

Reasons for Doing Right: The need to be a

good person in your own eyes and those of others; belief in the Golden Rule; desire to maintain rules and authority that support stereotypical good behavior.

Social Perspective of Stage: Perspective of the individual in relationships with other individuals. Aware of shared feelings, agreements, and expectations, which take primacy over individual interests. Relates points of view through the concrete Golden Rule, putting oneself in the other guy's shoes. Does not yet consider generalized system perspective.

Level and Stage:
Level II:
Stage 4: Social system and conscience.

What is Right: Fulfilling duties to which you have agreed; laws to be upheld except in extreme cases, where they conflict with other fixed social duties. *Right is also contributing to the society, group, or institution.*

Reasons for Doing Right: To keep the institution going as a whole and avoid a breakdown in the system. "If everyone did it" imperative of conscience to meet one's defined obligations (easily confused with stage 3 belief in rules and authority).

Social Perspective of Stage: Differentiates societal point of view from interpersonal agreement or motives. Takes the point of view of the system that defines roles and rules; considers individual relations in terms of place in the system.

Level and Stage:

Level III: Postconventional or Principled.
Stage 5: Social contract or utility and individual rights.

> *What is Right:* Being aware that people hold a variety of values and opinions and that most of their values and rules are relative to their group. Relative rules usually upheld in the interest of impartiality and because they are the social contract. Some nonrelative values and rights (e.g., life and liberty) must be upheld in any society and regardless of majority opinion.
>
> *Reason for Doing Right:* A sense of obligation to law because of one's social contract to make and abide by laws for the welfare of all and for the protection of all people's rights. A feeling of contractual commitment, freely entered upon, to family, friendship, trust, and work obligations. Concern that laws and duties be based on rational calculation of overall utility, "the greatest good for the greatest number."
>
> *Social Perspective of Stage:* Prior to society perspective—rational individuals aware of values and rights prior to social attachments and contracts. Integrates perspectives by formal mechanisms of agreement, contract, objective impartiality, and due process. Considers moral and legal points of view; recognizes that they sometimes conflict and finds it difficult to integrate them.

Level and Stage:

Level III
Stage 6: Universal ethical principles.

What is Right: Following self-chosen ethical principles. Particular laws or social agreements usually valid because they rest on such principles; when laws violate these principles, one acts in accordance with principle. Principles are universal principles of justice: equality of human rights and respect for the dignity of human beings as individuals.

Reasons for Doing Right: The belief as a rational person in the validity of universal moral principles and a sense of personal commitment to them.

Social Perspective of Stage: Perspective of a moral point of view from which social arrangements derive. Perspective is that of a rational individual recognizing the nature of morality of the fact that persons are ends in themselves and must be treated as such.[44]

According to Kohlberg's theory, a person's moral reasoning progresses through a series of developmental stages, with most of the adult population advancing to stage four, and very few, if any, reaching stage five or six. He suggests that the changes in moral development are independent of culture, social class, or religion, and that it is necessary for a person to achieve a lower stage before moving to a higher-order stage.

An example of this is a moral dilemma test devised by Kohlberg used to see at what moral stage a person is. The following is an example of a moral dilemma. In each stage, 1 through 6, answers and reasoning behind the answers are given.

In Europe, a woman was near death from cancer. One drug might save her, a form of radium that a druggist in the same town had recently discovered. The druggist was charging $2,000, ten times what the drug cost him to make. The sick woman's husband, Heinz, went to everyone he knew to borrow the money, but he could get together only about half of what the drug cost. He told the druggist that his wife was dying and asked him to sell the drug cheaper or let him pay later. But the druggist said "No." The husband got desperate and broke into the man's store to steal the drug for his wife. Should the husband have done that? Why or why not?

(Preventional Stage) Punishment and obedience orientation (physical consequences determine what is good or bad).

Stage 1

Pro: He should steal the drug. It isn't really bad to take it. It isn't like he didn't ask to pay for it first. The drug he'd take is only worth $200, he's not really taking a $2,000 drug.

Con: He shouldn't steal the drug. It's a big crime. He didn't get permission, he used force and broke-and-entered. He did a lot of damage stealing a very expensive drug and breaking up the store, too.

Instrumental relativism orientation (what satisfies one's own needs is good).

Stage 2

Pro: It's all right to steal the drug because she needs it and he wants her to live. It isn't that he wants to steal, but it's what he must do to get the drug to save her.

Con: He shouldn't steal it. The druggist isn't wrong or bad, he just wants to make a profit. That's what you're in business for, to make money.

(Conventional Stage) Interpersonal concordance or "good boy—nice girl" orientation; what pleases or helps others is good.)

Stage 3

Pro: He should steal the drug. He was only doing something that was natural for a good husband to do. You can't blame him for doing something out of love for his wife, you'd blame him if he didn't love his wife enough to save her.

Con: He shouldn't steal. If his wife dies, he can't be blamed. It isn't because he's heartless or that he doesn't love her enough to do everything that he legally can. The druggist is the selfish or heartless one.

"Law and order" orientation maintaining the social order, doing one's duty is good.

Stage 4

Pro: He should steal it. If he did nothing he'd be letting his wife die, it's his responsibility if she dies. He has to take it with the idea of paying the druggist.

Con: It is a natural thing for Heinz to want to save his wife, but it's still always wrong to steal. He still knows he's stealing and taking a valuable drug from the man who made it.

Post Conventional Stage: Social contract legalistic orientation (values agreed on by society, including individual rights and rules for consensus, determining what is right).

Stage 5

Pro: The law wasn't set up for these circumstances. Taking the drug in this situation isn't really right, but it's justified to do it.

Con: You can't completely blame someone for stealing, but extreme circumstances don't really justify taking the law into your own hands. You can't have everyone stealing whenever they get desperate. The end may be good, but the ends don't justify the means.

Universal ethical principle orientation (what is right is a matter of conscience in accord with universal principles.

Stage 6

Pro: This is a situation which forces him to choose between stealing and letting his wife die. In a situation where the choice must be made, it is morally right to steal. He has to act in terms of the principle of preserving and respecting life.

Con: Heinz is faced with the decision of whether to consider the other people who need the drug just as badly as his wife. Heinz ought to act not according to his particular feelings toward his wife, but considering the value of all lives involved.[45]

---

*(Source: Description of Kohlberg's stages from Shaver and Strong, 1976. Dilemma and pro and con answers from Rest, 1968).

After a student has finished taking this "Moral Dilemmas" test, Kohlberg would be able to determine what stage of moral thinking a person was in. He believed that each individual progressed through each stage sequentially.

As the student was exposed to more advanced moral reasoning, he would advance to a higher level. According to Kohlberg, each stage builds on the previous. Since Kohlberg's theory is "value free," there is no right or wrong; it's the moral reasoning the student uses to make a decision that is important. Kohlberg believes that a person's moral thinking changes when he is confronted with difficult moral dilemmas, and someone at a more advanced stage helps him advance to the next thinking stage. He stated that reorganizing and restructuring one's thinking increases when the person has more social interaction.

Since God is totally left out of this theory, and this concept is being taught indirectly throughout our schools, is it any wonder why we are experiencing a moral dilemma?

Analyzing moral dilemmas can be a good growth experience for any child. But, when the intention of the activity is to "shape" or "change" a person's value system, that is wrong. The following moral dilemmas are given to "gifted" junior and senior high students. The dilemmas are divided into different scenarios and students are to analyze and come up with a creative conclusion.

1. You are a civics teacher, discussing first amendment rights. It occurs to you the movie *Good Morning Vietnam* reflects the very issues you've been discussing. Since the movie carries an "R" rating, you ask your principal's permission to show

the movie. He concurs, if you send home permission slips. When you receive the permission slips back, only 45 percent say yes. Since the principal only asked you to send home slips and said nothing about percentages of yes responses, you must decide whether to show the movie, since it is obvious most parents do not wish you to. Will you show it or not? Why?[46]

2. You are a ten-year-old. Your father and mother are divorced, and you live with your mother. Your mentor, your father figure substitute, is a crusty old gentlemen in his seventies. He's been known to be drunk in public, and sometimes you don't understand his jokes. Your mother says that's because they're "dirty." But, he talks to you and takes you fishing and lets you eat whatever you want, whenever you want. Yesterday, your mother said you cannot see him any more. You know he depends on you for daily conversation, and you need his companionship. Will you obey your mother?[47]

3. Your best friend since second grade dies suddenly. You are in your forties. Your friend's family are fundamentalist Christians who don't even believe in dancing and view funerals as a solemn, spiritual occasion. Your friend, at odds with his family, loved a cute joke and even danced once in a while. As his dearest friend, you've been asked to give the eulogy. You want your friend remembered for his warmth and humor, but you know your remembrances of him may offend or even shock his family. What will you do?[48]

4. As the curator for a state-funded museum, you have managed to put together a marvelous collection of one artist. Recently, this now world-

famous artist died, making the museum's collection priceless. Because your museum had the best retrospective of his work, your museum has been asked to display his last work, *The Crude Nude*. You see the painting's artistic value and humor. You know others may not. In fact, there is a nation-wide movement to stop funding "obscene" art. Can you find a way to display the painting and keep your funding?[49]

Are these moral dilemmas that students face every day, or is this an attack on the Christian moral value system? I believe the latter is true.

With values clarification and Kohlberg's moral theory embedded in our schools and society, Christians need to step forward and be the decisive element that brings about change. Through each individual's personal approach, we will create change in our schools and communities.

As a Christian in today's diverse society, it is our response to the failing system that will create the change needed to put us back on track.

SEVEN

The Old Value System Re-examined

The search for a clarification of values is indicative of the spiritual/moral void that exists in our society. Perhaps we should commend ethicists, social scientists, and others for attempting to find a common reference point by which we, as a society, might treat one another with justice and mercy. The system to be agreed upon must consist of some principles beyond these two. It must be universally applicable, and yet unique in its superiority over presently inadequate systems. It must be consistent and easily understood. Simplicity is the key to both acceptance and compliance. It must be objective, not subjective. Finally, the end result of an applied system of values is a sense of peace.

The questions to be answered are: Does such a system exist? Can it be effectively communicated? If so, will it work?

We live in a society that questions the existence of moral absolutes. Students are encouraged to question, but often given little direction to solutions. In the eyes of some, this would be prejudicial education. "You can't have your cake and eat it, too." Schools have clearly determined some acceptable and unacceptable behavior. Drugs are forbidden, as are weapons. Attendance is mandatory. Yet, while these regulations are considered acceptable, the teaching of drug abstinence in many drug education programs is not. This is left for the child to decide after hearing information on drug usage.

This system is confusing to young people and must be extremely difficult for teachers. If moral absolutes do not exist, then anarchy should be acceptable, courts unjust, and each individual the ultimate reference point for universal truth. What a mixed message. Abstain from sex, but get your condoms in the nurse's office. Don't drink, but if you do, don't drive. It is my hope, that as the present generation matures, they will see the folly of our present moral system and will once again search for ultimate universal truth. Moral relativism leads to immorality.

We don't need values clarification! We need to demonstrate values. The public school has been given the mandate to teach reading, writing, and arithmetic. Parents have been given the responsibility of instilling morality. The unfair position teachers have been forced in is making them look like the bad guys. Not true. Society has abdicated its role, the family and church, in particular, as the source of moral absolutes. We need look no further for blame. Never has it been more true that our children are a reflection of us and our standards.

If we had the authority to design a moral system, what would it look like? How would it function? Perhaps, we should first determine if such a system already exists.

Justice

We are surrounded by injustice and suffering. Prejudice exists against color, height, and weight—fed by a media that in commentaries proclaim that color should not matter, then advertises tanning lotions. A sitcom about the unfairness of job discrimination due to weight is peppered by ads for various liquid diets. During dinner, the news features nations plagued by dysentery and famine: We watch an emaciated child too weak to even brush the flies from his eyes and mouth— suffering, pain, injustice.

It's all around. We need not travel far—child abuse down the block. On the corner, a nursing home with residents patiently awaiting the yearly visit by a stream of church groups singing "Joy to the World." The last carolers' echo has to hold them over until next Christmas. Nationally-known religious leaders fall in disgrace. Politicians are videotaped using drugs or taking payoffs.

Church memberships decline, and gangs grow. That which was unquestionably perverse is now called an acceptable lifestyle. Suicide statistics are increasing dramatically, especially among the elderly. The main export of some countries is drugs.

Where is the justice?

The drug dealer is sometimes back on the street before the police officer has finished the paperwork. A habitually violent criminal is released because of minor technicalities and overcrowded facilities. A child molester is never arrested: he abused numerous children, but the statute of limitations has expired.

Where is the justice?

An entire family is killed in an instant by a drunk driver. A ten-year-old dies of AIDS in his father's arms after contracting the disease from a tainted blood supply. Small children die in a house fire while mom steps out just long enough to get the mail.

Where is the justice? Why the suffering? Isn't it interesting that even those who practice no professed faith look to the heavens for an answer? "If there were a God, why would this happen?" Why should we even consider a value system based on a God who allows such unfathomable pain? Would another system without God change any of this?

Justice is where it has always been—with God. Children starve not because there is not enough soil to grow grain; man refuses to distribute to those in need, or he gouges the market with exorbitant prices that the poor cannot afford. Man often stands between God's grace and its intended recipient. There are those who claim that wars are the result of the world's religions. Let us not confuse man's interpretation of Scripture and God's intent. What about the 6 million Jews and Christians executed by the Nazi regime?

Perhaps this story best explains. A visitor to an infamous concentration camp was incensed, hurt, and confused—desperate to find an answer to the unexplainable! He scribbled on the prison wall, "Where was God?" in his utter exasperation. Sometime later, another visitor added his graffiti,

"Where was man?" We blame God for Satan's, or man's, actions. In so doing, we forget that God is the giver of every good and perfect gift (James 1:17).

Suffering is always the result of sin, inherent in human nature. A young passenger dies in a fiery car wreck because the driver broke the laws of nature that say speed, the weight of a car, and a dangerous curve do not mix. A child dies of heroin addiction at two months of age because of the sin of a parent.

My father died several years ago, and I preached at his funeral. At the beginning, I posed the question: "Where was God when my father died?" I believe that I shared the list of His spiritually eternal achievements and kept raising the question: "Where He always was, with my father, even in the 'valley of the shadow of death.'" My God never deserted my father. And He is still with him. The resurrection is God's answer to Satan and his plan for death and suffering. To the Christian, death is a temporary separation from living loved ones. It is not an enemy to those who suffered. My father is in a far better place. Even though we mourn now, we do not "mourn as those who have no hope" (I Thess. 4:13).

If death were the end, God would not be just. But, it isn't, and He is.

An argument against the evolution theory, as popularly proposed, is that man is not becoming morally superior to previous generations. If anything, we see a moral degeneration of society. Yet our schools decry injustice and argue a Darwinian theory of individual and societal evolution, devoid of a moral barometer. Sometimes I wonder if God sees the standard ape-to-man evolution chart displayed in school and wonders which end is the starting point. It is no wonder our inner cities are referred to as jungles, when the inhabitants act more like animals than as humans created in His divine image.

Simplicity

In His Word, God gave just ten commandments. They are a religious and ethical code. They are necessary to hold a society together. Mankind is a social creature as evidenced by God's divine discernment that Adam should have a suitable help mate. Humans were created with the capability to reproduce, assuring continued society. Any society—as large as the world community, or as small as a family—requires rules for cooperation. Preservation is dependent on simple rules.

Some religions have volumes of commentaries on numerous texts on what is moral, what isn't, and what falls into the "grey area" of interpretation. Various philosophies argue that there is no moral standard, that it changes with time and culture, or that it is strictly a matter of individual conscience. Debates rage on ethical issues—from war to abortion, euthanasia to homosexuality. Reams of paper continually roll off presses espousing the latest acceptable moral conduct. Jesus alone, with His divine wisdom, needed not expound or expand endlessly on proper moral conduct. His concept of values clarification was to "boil" the Ten Commandments down to the all-inclusive Golden Rule (Matt. 22:37-40).

Simple—the one who loves God, will love others. As Christians, we seek not a selfish solution, but a selfless one, knowing that our brothers and sisters seek to do the same. "Love your neighbor as yourself" implies two commands. The first is to love oneself, not because of what we do, but who we are, children of the King.

The story is told that a slave ship arrived and unloaded its human cargo. The shackled slaves were led onto a platform to be auctioned to the highest bidder. One particular slave mounted the steps and emanated an air of confidence, assurance, and self-respect. Unlike the others, though, his back bore the scars of numerous beatings. His back was not bowed, or head slumped. One plantation owner made this observation to a bidding friend. The friend replied, "He is proud; his father is a king in his homeland." Self-respect is simple as that.

Karl Barth, the eminent theologian, was asked to share his most profound spiritual insight. As the press anxiously awaited and anticipated a long, complex response, he simply said, "Jesus loves me." It's that simple. We love others because He first loved us (I John 4:10).

Ask those who have lived a long, full life about what made it most meaningful. They will give you examples of love expressed in the simplest ways: a garden flower, holding hands, the hug of a grandchild. Henry David Thoreau was correct—"Simplify, Simplify." Real learning is not accumulation of new information, it is most often unlearning false ideas.

Consistency

For two thousand years, men have tried to find fault with God's moral laws, and foolish men still seek to find a chink in the armor of God. When science or history and the Bible conflict, guess who wins. Evidences for the integrity and reliability of the Bible are critical to whether it should be considered a moral guide. Aside from the religious or spiritual focus of God's Word, it has ethics that few would reject.

Morality is not relativistic. That belief fosters the concept of an ever-changing base of morality which is unique yet superior.

Many moral/religious codes are unique, but not superior. Some demand that by cutting off the hands of a thief, we solve a problem. But, those systems can't be productive or provide restitution—both elements critical to justice.

Objectivity—not Subjectivity

The statue of Lady Justice is blind—not blind to evidence, but blind to clothing, cars, rings, looks, family trees, and other factors that make the judicial system unfair. Those who have money can afford to hire the best lawyers. Two problems with values clarification is that there is no standard, clear value. The ideal judge is one who can judge without any bias. Is that humanly possible? Indeed not. All of us carry biases and prejudices. That is human. We fight them and even sometimes suppress them, but they are there. Even a blind judge can be influenced by voice accent, or the use of proper or improper grammar. The standard of judgment I desire would be totally without human involvement!

God's Peace

Biblical peace is often misunderstood. It is not an absence of strife. Quite the contrary, biblical peace is lasting. The Christian can be at peace in the middle of a storm. Jesus slept while the Sea of Galilee raged around Him. So can we. Never should we allow circumstances to control us. In the deepest depression, Jesus is there. "Lo I am with you always, even unto the end of the age" (Matt.28:28). Even when human justice fails, and an innocent man is sent to prison, his reputation among men destroyed, God is just. His relationship to God is unchanged. If not in this life, in the next, justice—perfect justice—will prevail; God will not be mocked.

As I related earlier, I recently had an unexpected heart attack. Chest pains were misdiagnosed as "bronchial attacks." Before having my quadruple bypass, while I was awaiting the anesthesia, I remember a peace that "passes all understanding" (Phil. 4:7).

God's Value System

Mankind is God's greatest creation, and he wants to be with Him. God has devised a justice system that allows mankind to establish an eternal relationship with Him. This relationship rejects equality with God and separation from Him (deity of man and reincarnation, as taught by the New Age). We determine our eternal sentence based on justice and results of service to others: Matthew 25 (note Jesus' five questions) tempered with God's mercy and grace. No one really wants true justice, for "all have sinned and fallen short of the glory of God" (Rom. 3:23). We rely on grace (defined as all that God gives us, which we don't deserve) and mercy (all that God withholds from us, which we do deserve).

God expects me to teach and demonstrate godly morality, and I expect schools and all other public institutions to respect my values. The world has little to teach me of godly morality. It is time that we fan the flame on the candle set on the hill to warn the world!

The ultimate answer for those of us who hold a divine standard of morals is not idle conversation, but a convicting lifestyle that results in the world's conversion.

The Source of Morality

Have you ever considered the origin of your conscience? Some would argue that it's strictly the result of social dictates; that we are educated by our parents, teachers, churches; and that this forms our conscience. Immanuel Kant, the philosopher, in his *Critique of Pure Reason*, argued "Two things fill the mind with. . . admiration and awe. . . the starry heavens above and the moral law within."

He referred to this as an innate "sense of ought." Why would a person have deep concerns when he fails to follow his conscience, even at the earliest of ages? Could it be that we are born with a "sense of ought"? Is conscience innate? Would a child, abandoned on an island, grow up with a conscience? I think he most certainly would. This being the case, mustn't there be a moral governor of the universe—God?

C.S. Lewis argued that if we know evil is evil there must be a standard. In his *Mere Christianity*, Lewis presents a dilemma. As you pass by an ocean and notice a victim drowning, you have two impulses: to dive in and help save the man's life, and also, a desire to avoid risking your own life. However, Lewis continues, "You will find inside you, in addition to these two impulses, a third thing which tells you that you ought to follow the impulse to help, and suppress the impulse to run away."

Some might argue that man is not consistent in his moral decisions from moment to moment, but that simply indicates that we are not automatons, the by-product of evolutionary chance. We are not merely matter, but moral agents with the ability to reason and make choices. The Source or Author of morality is a divine designer.

Assuming there is a moral design innate in each of us, and that its source is a moral God, how would He reveal the specifics of this code? Throughout time, the Judeo-Christian God has chosen to reveal Himself to man through the Word. History can be divided in four periods: the Creation, the Revelation, the Incarnation, and the Resurrection. In each of these four epochs, we have evidence of the Word of God. In the first, God spoke exnihilo—from nothing—to create the Universe.

Second, he gave His divine revelations to mankind in the garden, then to his people directly through Abraham and others. As society increased numerically, God saw fit to codify His directives. The Ten Commandments were meant to be the written word that dictated how man was to live. The first four have to do with man's relationship and responsibility to God. The last six deal with man's relationship to man. Thus, spirituality and morality clearly are not meant to be separated.

Third, He spoke through His Son, coming "in the flesh." This is referred to as the incarnation. "His Word became flesh and dwelt among us" (John 1:14). He demonstrated perfect morality based on a correct relationship to God. Finally, at His call, there will be a resurrection of the faithful, and once again, He will communicate with us directly. God has and always will reveal His will to us through His Word. This Word, however, must be infallible, without error. For four thousand years, it has stood the test.

EIGHT

"What Is Truth?"

This book is not meant to be an emotional appeal to reject the things of Satan and turn to the one true and living God. Some of us, myself included, need concrete evidence for making a major lifestyle change. Faith built solely on emotion is like a house built on a foundation of sand: "And the rain descended, and the floods came, and the winds blew, and burst against that house; and it fell and great was its fall" (Matt. 7:27).

Faith without logic is also akin to the point of Jesus' parable found in Luke 8:4-15. Jesus explains this lesson. He describes that the seed planted in rocky soil "are those who, when they hear, receive the word with joy, and these have no firm root; they believe for a while, and in time of temptation fall away" (Luke 8:13). Some professing Christian denominations reflect the full spectrum. Some, at least by example, reject the use of the God-given ability to reason and rely largely on emotion. At the other end of the spectrum, there are those who claim that God reveals Himself solely through

His Word, the Bible, and God-given emotions are to be suppressed, if not ignored. Historically, the pendulum of reason and emotion has seldom paused in the middle. Both are from God and are meant to "compliment" one another.

The world looks at a fragmented Church and asks, "What Is Truth?"—a valid question and one asked with particular poignancy two thousand years ago. Jesus, while praying late at night in the Garden of Gethsemane, is approached by an armed gang led by Roman soldiers, Jewish leaders, and a man named Judas Iscariot. Three years previously, Judas had been chosen by Jesus to be one of the select twelve. He was even given responsibility for the apostolic treasury (John 12:4-6). Now, as a prearranged signal, he approaches Jesus and kisses Him. The kiss, a symbol of deep affection, is seen now as the ultimate act of betrayal.

It is interesting to note that in the Greek, the word is much more explicit. It means to kiss effusively, over and over again. Not a simple peck to the cheek or forehead. Jesus is led away to various trials. Standing before Pilate, Jesus spoke, "My Kingdom is not of this world. If my Kingdom were of this world, then my servants would be fighting, that I might not be delivered up to the Jews."

Pilate, therefore, said to Him, "So you are a King?" Jesus answered, "You say correctly that I am a King. For this I have been born, and for this I have come into the world, to bear witness to the truth. Everyone who is of the truth hears my voice."

Pilate said to Him, "What is truth?" And when he had said this, he went out again to the Jews and said to them (the crowd), "I find no guilt in Him."

Pilate was acknowledging that he had confronted Truth. Peer pressure, prestige, and a weak backbone caused Pilate to reject it. Instead, he tried to absolve his own guilt by washing his hands in an attempt to remove the stain of an innocent man's blood. It didn't work then, anymore than for Lady MacBeth, or anyone who comes in contact with Jesus and rejects Him. History tells us that the Jews later turned against Pilate, and tradition tells us that he died by his own hand. Perhaps he could never come to deal with his part in the killing of Truth.

The point of this chapter is not to intellectually establish the divinity of Christ (this was done many years ago), but instead, to respond to the question, if the Word of God is the moral guide and the ultimate of all clarified values, is it practical? Is it possible to take these values and successfully apply them in our world—a world already established, as being decadent, crying for moral leaders? I present Jesus, for the sake of argument, a historic figure who had to deal with ethnic prejudices, sexual biases, geographical and territorial disputes, the question of social status, legalism, and forgiveness.

If, indeed, "the Word became flesh and dwelt among us" (John 1:14), how would He deal with the continuing and ever present problems of humanity? If truth were skin, how would it act? Are we not all looking for a real moral role model? I see it everyday with young people being ever increasingly attracted to the occult—satanism in particular. Without exception, male and female, they all express the absence of a role model (especially a male role model). All our heroes have fallen.

Political heroes end up with major character flaws, preachers' weaknesses are publicly displayed. Where are we to look for a consistent example of morality in dealing with life situations that face us daily?

Geographical and Territorial Dispute

John 4:3-26

> He left Judea and set out once more for Galilee. He had to pass through Samaria, and on his way came to a Samaritan town called Sychar, near the plot of ground that Jacob gave to his son Joseph; Jacob's well was there. It was about noon, and Jesus, tired after his journey, was sitting by the well.
>
> His disciples had gone into the town to buy food. Meanwhile a Samaritan woman came to draw water, and Jesus said to her, "Give me a drink."
>
> The woman said, "What? You, a Jew, ask for a drink from a Samaritan woman?" (Jews do not share drinking vessels with Samaritans.)
>
> Jesus replied, "If only you knew what God gives, and who it is that is asking you for a drink, you would have asked him and he would have given you living water."
>
> "Sir," the woman said, 'you have no bucket and the well is deep, so where can you get 'living water'? Are you greater than Jacob our ancestor who gave us the well and drank from it himself, he and his sons and his cattle too?"
>
> Jesus answered, "Everyone who drinks this water will be thirsty again; but whoever drinks the water I shall give will never again be thirsty.

The water that I shall give will be a spring of water within him, welling up and bringing eternal life."

"Sir," said the woman, "give me this water, and then I shall not be thirsty, nor have to come all this way to draw water."

"Go and call your husband," said Jesus, "and come back here." She answered, "I have no husband." Jesus said, "You are right in saying that you have no husband, for though you have had five husbands, the man you are living with now is not your husband. You have spoken the truth!"

"Sir," replied the woman, "I can see you are a prophet. Our fathers worshipped on this mountain, but you Jews say that the place where God must be worshipped is in Jerusalem."

"Believe me," said Jesus, "the time is coming when you will worship the Father neither on this mountain nor in Jerusalem. You Samaritans worship you know not what; we worship what we know. It is from the Jews that salvation comes. But the time is coming, indeed it is already here, when true worshippers will worship the Father in spirit and in truth. These are the worshippers the Father wants. God is spirit, and those who worship him must worship in spirit and in truth."

The woman answered, "I know that Messiah" (that is, Christ) is coming. When he comes he will make everything clear to us."

Jesus said to her, "I am He, I who am speaking to you."

None would argue that wars rage around the world. Excuses are given, treaties are broken and long-term peace seldom exists. Many of these disputes are less over ground and more over contrasting belief systems. We need look no further than the Middle East. For thousands of years, men on both sides, convinced that God is on their side, have killed one another. This part of the world has never known peace.

Even within the Jewish world at the time of Jesus, there were disputes interprovincially. Jesus was born in Galilee; this province was not considered a Jewish religious center. Judea, however, was thought to be the "hub" of the Jewish faith. Here, Jerusalem, "the city of peace," sat perched atop a hill. The temple, God's earthly dwelling place, was to Jews what Mecca was to become to Moslems. It was, and is, the lifelong goal and ambition of every Jew to return to Jerusalem. Some Jews felt that merely living in Judea meant that they were spiritually superior to Jews in the other provinces.

No people were looked down on more than the inhabitants of the middle province, Samaria. The Samaritans of Jesus' day were the result of inter-marriage of members of the ten tribes with non-Jews who entered the area after Samaria fell in 722 B.C. By marrying outside the Jewish heritage, they were considered spiritual apostates. Other Jews would avoid passing through this province on their journeys, even if it meant a longer trip. As they went north from Judea or south from Galilee, most would bypass Samaria by crossing to the eastern bank of the Jordan River.

The Samaritans had established Mount

Gerizim "the mount of Blessing," as their holy mount, an alternative to Jerusalem (Deut. 27:12). Here, they built their own temple when the Jews who returned from captivity refused them permission to help in reconstructing the temple in Jerusalem.

In John's Gospel, Jesus is recorded as traveling from Judea to Galilee. He passed through Samaria and stopped at the city of Sychar. One of Jacob's wells was located here, and Jesus wearily approached it and sat on its stone ledge. It was near dawn, and as Jesus waited, a Samaritan woman approached to draw water. Jesus asked her for a drink. Jews did not talk to Samaritans; Jesus did. He was breaking an ethnic taboo. Her reply, "How is it that you, being a Jew, ask me for a drink since I am a Samaritan woman?" The main point of this encounter was not simply over water, but of relationships. Jesus was interested in her, not her heritage. He was seeking to tear down the walls, not continue to build them.

Many today talk about Christians being intolerant. Unfortunately, this is often true. But, our leader set an example. His tolerance is my model. We can extend this example to those with whom we have contact in our everyday lives. For whom do we have the greatest ethnic hate? Some in every culture or race have their scapegoats as the answer to the ills of the world. Jesus appealed to common traits and characteristics, not differences. It was Jesus' first goal to establish a relationship with whomever he came in contact. He sought similarities, not differences. Keep in mind that He didn't agree with everything that these individuals believed, but the greatest lasting changes come from within, as the result of seeing an example. Jesus chose not to alienate, but love. Love motivates change. He was the true demonstration of love, the resolution of conflict.

New Agers advocate sending out vibratory messages of peace—the more of us sending this psychic vibration, the better the chances are of world peace and harmony. This "harmonic convergence" is even advocated by some New Agers as the answer to prisoner rehabilitation.

The biblical response to enemies is to love them and to go one step further, to pray for those who persecute you (Matt. 5:44). Jesus demonstrates what it means to love your enemies. In Matthew 5:23-24, Jesus talks about the moral responsibility of one who has offended another: "If your eyes are bad, your whole body will be in darkness. If then the only light you have is darkness, how great a darkness that will be."

Jesus makes it clear that our relationship to God is also dependent on our relationship to one another. But, what about the one offended? Does he have any moral responsibility for reconciliation? Again, listen to the words of Jesus in Matthew 18:15-20: "If your brother does wrong, go and take the matter up with him, strictly between yourselves. If he listens to you, you have won your brother over. But if he will not listen, take one or two others with you, so that every case may be settled on the evidence of two or three witnesses. If he refuses to listen to them, report the matter to the congregation; and if he will not listen even to the congregation, then treat him as you would a pagan or a tax-collector.

"Truly I tell you, whatever you forbid on earth

shall be forbidden in heaven, and whatever you allow on earth shall be allowed in heaven.

"And again I tell you, if two of you agree on earth about any request you have to make, that request will be granted by my heavenly Father. For where two or three meet together in my name, I am there among them."

Jesus makes it clear that, whether we are the offender or offendee, we both are morally responsible. The ideal is that these two individuals would meet on the roads somewhere between their two homes. Jesus' morality was practical, He states the logical. This simple step is sometimes not sufficient. So, He presents non-overactive steps to seek reconciliation. Those with whom I have talked, who question the efficacy of such a remedy have not tried it. The church has feared demonstrating church discipline because, in the process, it often forgets its purpose—restoration. Discipline must always be motivated by love, not retribution.

Legalism

We face narrow-minded individuals every day at work, in our neighborhood, in school, and even in our churches. It's frustrating! How can we so clearly see the inconsistencies in other people and, at the same time, be so blinded by our own? The Jews at the time of Jesus, were splintered into a wide spectrum of sects—from ultra-liberal to ultra-conservative.

For example, the Old Testament gives short prohibition concerning work on the Sabbath in Exodus 16:23-30, 20:8-11, 23:12, 31:12-17, 34:21, and 35:1-3. The early rabbis felt that God's Word was not specific enough, so various schools of

Torah interpretation saw it necessary to define
work more precisely. The following is a list of
thirty-nine kinds of work that were to be prohibited on the Sabbath (from *The Jewish People in the
Time of Christ* by Emil Schurer, T & T Clark,
Edinburgh, Scotland, 1890, p. 97): (1) sowing, (2)
ploughing, (3) reaping, (4) binding sheaves, (5)
threshing, (6) winnowing, (7) cleansing crops, (8)
grinding, (9) sifting, (10) kneading, (11) baking,
(12) shearing wool, (13) washing, (14) beating,
(15) dyeing, (16) spinning, and (17) warping it,
(18) making two cords, (19) weaving two threads,
(20) separating two threads, (21) making a knot,
(22) untying a knot, (23) sewing two stitches, (24)
tearing to sew two stitches, (25) catching a deer,
(26) killing, (27) skinning, (28) salting it, (29) preparing its skin, (30) scraping off the hair, (31)
cutting it up, (32) writing two letters, (33) blotting
out of the purpose of writing two letters, (34)
building, (35) pulling down, (36) putting out a
fire, (37) lighting a fire, (38) beating smooth with
a hammer, (39) carrying from one tenement to
another.

By establishing a specific list, one is begging
for confusion. Other rabbinical scholars carried
this step further. On pages 98 and 99 of the same
book is the following: "The following are the knots,
the making of which renders a man guilty: The
knot of camel-drivers and that of sailors; and as
one is guilty by reason of tying, so also of untying
them."

R. Meir says that guilt is not incurred by reason of a knot that can be untied with one hand.
There are knots by reason of which one is not
guilty, as one is in the cads of the camel-driver's
and sailor's knots. A woman may tie up a slit in

her shift and the strings of her cap, those of her girdle, the straps of the shoes and sandals, of skins of wine and oil, of a pot with meat. And to tie strings of the girdle being permitted, it was agreed that a pail also might be tied over the well with a girdle, but not with a rope.

The prohibition of writing on the Sabbath was further defined as follows:

He who writes two letters with his right or his left hand, whether of one kind or of two kinds, as also if they are written with different ink or are of different languages, is guilty. He even who should from forgetfulness write two letters is guilty, whether he has written them with ink or with paint, re chalk, India-rubber, vitriol, or anything which makes permanent marks. Also he who writes on two walls which form an angle, or on the two tablets of his account-book, so that they can be read together, is guilty. He who writes upon his body is guilty. If any one writes with dark fluid, with fruit juice, or in the dust on the road, in sand, or in anything in which the writing does not remain, he is free. If any one writes with the wrong hand, with the foot, with the mouth, with the elbow; also if any one writes upon a letter of another piece of writing, or covers other writing; also if any one meaning to write has only written two, or if any one has written one letter on the ground and one upon the wall, or upon two walls of the house, or upon two pages of a book, so that they cannot be read together, he is free. If in forgetfulness he writes two letters at different times, perhaps one in the morning and one towards evening, R. Gamaliel pronounces him guilty, the learned declare him free.

In order to get around these manmade regulations, Jews devised devious interpretations. To avoid carrying a burden further than 7/10 mile, beyond which on Sabbath would be prohibited, some would carry a pouch of meaningless items, drop one every 7/10 mile, which allowed them to go further. The more conservative Jews insisted that sandals held together by small nails could not be worn on the Sabbath. By so doing, each step was literally lifting nails, or working on the Sabbath!

If, as New Agers claim, we are God, how do we explain our foolishness? It is one thing to lie to another, but to lie to ourselves is the epitome of self-destruction. Would God lie to Himself? Once again, Jesus is our example. He examined accurately the intent and hearts of men and realized their humanity. How could Jesus identify with this state of humanity?

Hebrews 2:17, 18;4:15: "Therefore he had to be made like his brothers in every way, so that he might be merciful and faithful, their high priest before God, to make expiation for the sins of the people. Because He Himself has passed through the test of suffering, He is able to help those who are in the midst of their test.

"Ours is not a high priest unable to sympathize with our weaknesses, but one who has been tested in every way as we are, only without sinning."

Though fully divine, He was fully human. This concept is beyond the perimeters of this book. Remember, we are focusing on how Jesus, the man, dealt with moral dilemmas. At this point, we are examining the rules imposed by men that separate him from God.

Jesus specifically addressed this dogma that breeds separation and divisiveness in Luke 11:37-54:

> When he had finished speaking, a Pharisee invited him to a meal, and he came in and sat down. The Pharisee noticed with surprise that he had not begun by washing before the meal. But the Lord said to him, "You Pharisees clean the outside of the cup and plate; but inside you are full of greed and wickedness. You fools! Did not He who made the outside make the inside too? But let what is inside be given in charity, and all is clean.

> "Alas for you Pharisees! You pay tithes of mint and rue and every garden herb, but neglect justice and the love of God. It is these you should have practiced, without overlooking the other.

> "Alas for you Pharisees! You love to have the chief seats in synagogues, and to be greeted respectfully in the street.

> "Alas, alas, you are like unmarked graves which people walk over unawares.

> "At this one of the lawyers said, "Teacher, when you say things like this you are insulting us too." Jesus rejoined: "Alas for you are lawyers also! You load men with intolerable burdens, and will not lift a finger to lighten the load.

> "Alas, you build monuments to the prophets whom your fathers murdered, and so testify that you approve of the deeds your fathers did; they committed the murders and you provide the monuments.

> "This is why the Wisdom of God said, 'I will send them prophets and messengers; and

some of these they will persecute and kill;' so that this generation will have to answer for the blood of all the prophets shed since the foundation of the world; from the blood of Abel to the blood of Zechariah who met his death between the altar and the sanctuary. I tell you, this generation will have to answer for it all.

"Alas for you lawyers! You have taken away the key of knowledge. You did not go in yourselves, and those who were trying to go in, you prevented.

After he had left the house, the scribes and Pharisees began to assail him fiercely and to ply him with a host of questions, laying snares to catch him with his own words.

Jesus became angry! Yes, angry! With Jesus as an example, we are to be angry over injustice and prejudice and divisiveness. What makes us angry is one indicator of our spiritual growth. We are to be angry in a righteous manner. We should not internalize our anger; we should not explode; we are not to be angry with people. We are to focus the God-given emotional energy of anger towards a solution. Jesus displayed a spirit of reconciliation. It is no accident that Paul refers to us as "ministers of reconciliation" (II Cor. 5:18).

Ethnic Prejudice

Luke 10:25-37:

A lawyer once came forward to test him by asking: "Teacher, what must I do to inherit eternal life?"

Jesus said, "What is written in the law? What is your reading of it?"

He replied, "Love the Lord your God with all your heart, and with all your souls, with all your strength, and with all your mind; and your neighbor as yourself."

"That is the right answer," said Jesus. "Do that and you will have life."

Wanting to justify his question, he asked, "But who is my neighbor?"

Jesus replied, "A man was on his way from Jerusalem down to Jericho when he was going down by the same road, and when he saw him, he went past on the other side. So too a Levite came to the place, and when he saw him went past on the other side. But a Samaritan who was going that way came upon him, and when he saw him he was moved to pity. He went up and bandaged his wounds, bathing them with oil and wine. Then he lifted him on to his own beast, brought him to an inn, and looked after him. Next day he produced two silver pieces and gave them to the innkeeper, and said, 'Look after him; and if you spend more, I will repay you on my way back.' Which of these three do you think was neighbor to the man who fell into the hands of the robbers?"

He answered, "The one who showed him kindness."

Jesus said to him, "Go and do as he did."

We have already mentioned the animosity that most Jews exhibited toward the Samaritans. Jesus here gives us a living example of how we are to react to those who hold different views. Remember that much bigotry is the result of instilled values, often inherited. It could be that these big-

ots have never been exposed to anything but those
who seem to reinforce the negative stereotypes.
Keep in mind Jesus doesn't say adapt all the characteristics of other people, or accept their false
religious beliefs; but He, once again, demonstrates
love to bring about the goal of reconciliation.
Imagine the shock of the Pharisees, Jesus demonstrating that the true neighbor was a Samaritan.

It is a sad commentary that there are those
who have not given themselves to God, are not
spiritual, and, yet, demonstrate a Christ-like love.
When Jesus returns, will He be shocked at our
narrow-minded attitude toward others. Has the
blind acceptance of negative stereotypes replaced
getting close enough to see people as they really
are? With hurt and hopes, pains and dreams, we
are all created in God's image! We are all children
of God! Some need to be shown by example what
the Father is like; they are estranged children who
need to be reconciled.

New Agers claim we are all related as well.
They mean, by this, that we are all God—a divine
entity, and we are related to the god in all nature.

In reply, only humans—of all God's creation—
are created in His image. It is a shame that truth
has become a cliche: "Hate the sin, but love the
sinner." My role model did just that. He understood our humanity, but sought to see each one of
us reach our potential—not as gods but as God's.
Jesus was not interested in a person's skin color;
He was totally consumed with reaching and filling
the vacuum in all men's heart.

Sexual Bias

John 8:1-11:

> But Jesus went to the Mount of Olives. At dawn he appeared again in the temple courts, where all the people gathered around him, and he sat down to teach them. The teachers of the law and the Pharisees brought in a woman caught in adultery. They made her stand before the group and said to Jesus, "Teacher, this woman was caught in the act of adultery. In the Law, Moses commanded us to stone such women. Now what do you say?" They were using this question as a trap, in order to have a basis for accusing him.

> But Jesus bent down and started to write on the ground with his finger. When they kept on questioning him, he straightened up and said to them, "If anyone of you is without sin, let him be the first to throw a stone at her." Again he stooped down and wrote on the ground.

> At this, those who heard began to go away one at a time, the older ones first, until only Jesus was left, with the woman still standing there. Jesus straightened up and asked her, "Woman, where are they? Has no one condemned you?"

> "No one, sir," she said.

> "Then neither do I condemn you," Jesus declared. "Go now and leave your life of sin." (verses taken from NIV)

At the time of Jesus, Jewish men would arise and recite the morning prayer, "Thank you God I was not born a slave, a Gentile, or a woman."

There were two basic schools of thought when it came to divorce. The strictest sect held that grounds for divorce included a burned meal and even unspecified dissatisfaction with a wife. Women were property. Women could not initiate divorce—that remained a male prerogative.

Jesus opened this up. He was extremely specific as to the grounds acceptable for divorce. It, thus, protected the woman and also allowed her the same privilege. As we have seen, Jesus addressed the Samaritan woman at the well. (In one act, He broke two social taboos.) It can be argued that of all religions, Christianity views women with the most respect. Mary was chosen to raise Jesus, the Messiah. Jesus conversed with women on numerous occasions, and among the list of those loyal in attending to His needs are a long list of faithful women. It was a woman who was chosen to be the first evangelist as she ran from His empty tomb proclaiming the Good News of the Gospel. On the cross, Jesus, in the midst of agony, made sure that John would take care of his mother.

Jesus respected women. He never ignored biological or emotional differences, but He never diminished the image of God in each woman. I find no scriptural evidence to support Jesus advocating the inferiority of women.

One story clearly points out Jesus' attitude. The Pharisees cared not for the woman caught in adultery. They were trying to trap Jesus, in violation not of blaspheming God and His dictates, but of their religious dogma. Deuteronomy 19:15 requires that in such immoral actions, two witnesses were unnecessary, but by not presenting them, the Pharisees, themselves, were ignoring God's dictation. The tantalizing question is what Jesus wrote on the ground. How ironic, that the only writing of Jesus during His earthly existence was blown away by the wind or trampled upon by the crowds. Speculation has run rampant, but the fact is, we don't know what He wrote. But, it greatly disturbed and disarmed the Pharisees who had brought this charge against the woman.

Could it be that Jesus revealed their personal sins, appropriately, in the dirt? He then challenged them, "He that is without sin, let him cast the first stone." The crowd dispersed.

Note also that the Pharisees ignored another biblical requirement that the male involved in this immoral act was to be stoned as well (Lev. 20:10). The Scripture states that she was caught in the very act; where was the man? Jesus saw the hypocrisy. After the crowd left, He dealt with her needs. She addressed Jesus with a title of respect. He could tell she was sorrowful, repentant, and obviously, thankful for Jesus' compassion. He doesn't ignore her act of sin, but He loves her and commands her to sin no more. I would hope that my brothers and sisters would confront me with my sin, but have the compassion to accept my repentance and grant me forgiveness. Jesus did, and He is my example.

New Agers make no sexual distinctions; that's denying reality.

Luke 7:36-50:

> One of the Pharisees invited Jesus to a meal; he went to the Pharisee's house and took his place at the table. A woman who was living an immoral life in the town learned that Jesus was a guest in the Pharisee's house and

brought oil of myrrh in a small flask. She took her place behind him, by his feet, weeping. His feet were wet with her tears, and she wiped them with her hair, kissing them and anointing them with the myrrh. When his host, the Pharisee, saw this, he said to himself, "If this man were a real prophet, he would know who this woman is who is touching him, and what a bad character she is." Jesus took him up, "Simon," he said, "I have something to say to you."

"What is it, Teacher?" he asked.

"Two men were in debt to a moneylender: one owed him five hundred silver pieces, the other fifty. As they did not have the means to pay, he canceled both debts. Now, which will love him more?"

Simon replied, "I should think the one that was let off more."

"You are right," said Jesus. Then turning to the woman, he said to Simon, "You see this woman? I came to your house: you provided no water for my feet, but she wet them with her tears and wiped them with her hair. You gave me no kiss; but she has been kissing my feet ever since I came in. You did not anoint my head with oil; but she has anointed my feet with myrrh. So, I tell you her great love proves that her many sins have been forgiven; where little has been forgiven, little love is shown." Then he said to her, "Your sins are forgiven." The other guests began to ask themselves, "Who is this, that he can forgive sins?" But he said to the woman, "Your faith has saved you; go in peace."

Once again, Jesus teaches us a lesson, not only on the treatment of women, but of all humans. It is established early on that all acknowledged this woman as a sinner. Jesus knew this but allowed her to attend to Him. In so doing, He was preparing a lesson for the bystanders and giving her an opportunity to demonstrate sorrow for her sin. She wept and, in respect, kissed His feet in a sincere display of true affection. Jesus then used a parable to explain forgiveness.

Simon, his host, had ignored the most expected aspects of hospitality. When a guest entered his host's home, his feet were washed since he had worn sandals travelling over dusty roads. The custom of kissing the cheeks of a guest was expected. Oil would be provided as a sign of honor and to comfort and cool the skin. Only this woman had shown respect. This sinful woman anointed Jesus with her valuable oil. Jesus told her that her sins are forgiven. She demonstrated sorrow and a desire to change her lifestyle.

Once again, Jesus deals with a moral dilemma. He faces the challenge, and all can leave victorious. The Pharisees, however, retreat for another battle.

Social Status

Jesus spoke frequently of the poor. He evaluated their social status. Let's not misunderstand. Jesus did not say being poor was superior. He does, however, make it clear that wealth and its accompanying possessions sometimes prevent us from understanding our dependence on God. Self-sufficiency is a dangerous thing. The poor realize the value of things that cannot be purchased—

love, friendship, family. Hopefully, they don't take for granted their last meal or expect their next. Jesus said it would be "easier for a camel to pass through the eye of a needle than for a rich man to enter into Heaven" (Matt. 19:24). Riches often obscure our spiritual vision.

Matthew 19:16-22:

> A man came up and asked him, "Teacher, what good must I do to gain eternal life?"
>
> "Good?" said Jesus. "Why do you ask me about that? God alone is good. But if you wish to enter into life, keep the commandments."
>
> "Which commandments?" he asked.
>
> Jesus answered, "Do not murder; do not commit adultery; do not steal; do not give false evidence; honor your father and mother; and love your neighbor as yourself."
>
> The young man answered, "I have kept all these. What do I still lack?" Jesus said to him, "If you wish to be perfect, go, sell your possessions, and give to the poor, and you will have treasure in heaven; then come and follow me."
>
> When the young man heard this, he went away with a heavy heart; for he was a man of great wealth.

The man approached Jesus, asking the most important question in life. The man asked what "thing" he must do to achieve salvation. Two men talking, but not communicating. One was worldly, the other truly spiritual. Jesus responds to the question by sharing the Golden Rule. Simply stated, the man was to establish a right relationship with God and a right relationship to his fellow man.

New Agers would insist that this is one and the same commandment. To be consistent, no New Ager could claim, as they do, that Jesus was an avatar (see chapter 3). To them, Jesus is inconsistent in this and many other passages in clarifying the distinction between man and God.

Jesus continues and presents the man with a moral dilemma (v. 21,22). Because he is unwilling to part with the security of his material goods, the young man leaves grieved. His riches had become so much a part of him, that his fear of losing that security was beyond the price he would pay, even for the most precious of all gifts. By helping the poor who needed his wealth—not to become wealthy but to survive, he would receive eternal life. Jesus cared for the sinful rich and the needy.

Matthew 25:31-46:

> When the Son of Man comes in his glory and all the angels with him, he will sit on his glorious throne, with all the nations gathered before him. He will separate people into two groups, as a shepherd separates the sheep from the goats; he will place the sheep on his right hand and the goats on his left.

> Then the king will say to those on his right, "You have my Father's blessing; come, take possession of the kingdom that has been ready for you since the world was made. For when I was hungry, you gave me food; when thirsty, you gave me drink; when I was a stranger, you took me into your home; when naked, you clothed me; when I was ill, you came to

my help; when in prison, you visited me."

Then the righteous will reply, "Lord when was it that we saw you hungry and fed you, or thirsty and gave you drink, a stranger and took you home, or naked and clothed you? When did we see you ill or in prison, and come to visit you?" And the king will answer, "Truly I tell you: anything you did for one of my brothers here, however insignificant, you did for me."

Then he will say to those on his left, "A curse is on you; go from my sight to the eternal fire that is ready for the devil and his angels. For when I was hungry, you gave me nothing to eat; when thirsty, nothing to drink; when I was a stranger, you did not welcome me; when I was naked, you did not clothe me; when I was ill and in prison, you did not come to my help." And they in their turn will reply, "Lord, when was it that we saw you hungry or thirsty or a stranger or naked or ill or in prison, and did nothing for you?" And he will answer, "Truly I tell you: anything you failed to do for one of these, however insignificant, you failed to do for me." And they will go away to eternal punishment, but the righteous will enter eternal life.

On the Day of Judgment, Jesus will ask five questions: Did you feed the hungry, give water to the thirsty, clothe the naked, visit the sick and those in prison? What statement is this making? Perhaps, the wealth we accumulate is given us so that we might be able to help those less fortunate.

New Agers, once again, show inconsistency. Many are yuppies, wealthy individuals who believe that, as gods, they deserve the best.

Unfortunately, we have Christians who believe that because they are Christians, they will be "healthy and wealthy." Ask Job if this theology makes sense. Ask Jesus, who died with only a robe to His name. Ask the Apostles, who gave even their lives, whether riches are always an indication of righteousness.

Luke 14:7-11:

> When he noticed how the guests were trying to secure the places of honor, he spoke to them in a parable: "When somebody asks you to a wedding feast, do not sit down in the place of honor. It may be that some person more distinguished than yourself has been invited; and the host will come to say to you, Give this man your seat. Then you will look foolish as you go to take the lowest place. No, when you receive an invitation, go and sit down in the lowest place, so that when your host comes he will say, Come up higher, my friend. Then all your fellow-guests will see the respect in which you are held. For everyone who exalts himself will be humbled, and whoever humbles himself will be exalted."

Jesus made it clear: the greatest of all is the servant. The world looks down upon servants. Jesus though came as a servant to show us what being truly human should be. He was not impressed by crowns and jewels.

There are New Agers who look down with disdain on those who fail to recognize the deity within them. There is, no doubt, a clear sense of prejudice against the "unsuccessful" in the terms of this world. In one breath they espouse unity and proclaim the divine intent of the diversity of the rainbow. In the next, they imply strongly that the rainbow is not strikingly distinct colors, but, rather, slightly variant shades of just a few. The New Ager is elitist.

My example, my role model of how to deal with social status, would cringe at this attitude; so, must I.

Luke 14:12-14:

> Then he said to his host, "When you are having guests for lunch or supper, do not invite your friends, your brothers or other relations, or your rich neighbors; they will only ask you back again, and so, you will be repaid. But when you give a party, ask the poor, the crippled, the lame, and the blind. That is the way to find happiness, because they have no means of repaying you. You will be repaid on the day when the righteous rise from the dead."

In this section of Scripture, Jesus reminds us that those with means have a moral responsibility to those less fortunate. Social conscience should dictate a deep desire to share. Our society has held the ideal of accumulation. Jesus wants us to realize that we should invest in the eternal future. Too often, when the wealthy are mentioned, most Americans think of a small minority of heirs to fortunes and unbelievably successful entrepreneurs. It's all relative. A vast majority of Americans are rich beyond comprehension, in comparison to the rest of the world. Jesus commended the poor widow who gave what she had. We need to be honest with ourselves. By continually saving, and refusing to share, are we not demonstrating in a

very concrete way, our lack of dependence upon
God?

Luke 14:15-24:

> Hearing this one of the company said to him,
> "Happy are those who will sit at the feast in
> the kingdom of God!"
>
> Jesus answered, "A man was giving a big din-
> ner party and had sent out many invitations.
> At dinner-time he sent his servant to tell his
> guests, 'Come please, everything is now ready.'
> One after another they all sent excuses. The
> first said, 'I have bought a piece of land, and
> I must go and inspect it; please accept my
> apologies.' The second said, 'I have bought
> five yoke of oxen, and I am on my way to try
> them out; please accept my apologies.' The
> next said, 'I cannot come; I have just gotten
> married,' When the servant came back he
> reported this to his master. The master of the
> house was furious and said to him, 'Go out
> quickly into the street and alleys of the town,
> and bring in the poor, the crippled, the blind,
> and lame.' When the servant informed him
> that his orders had been carried out and there
> was still room, his master replied, 'Go out on
> the highways and along the hedgerows and
> compel them to come in; I want my house
> full. I tell you, not one of those who were
> invited shall taste my banquet.'"

Those who have made money and its accumulation their goal soon find that anything that
does not further that goal is unnecessary. This
includes time to nurture relationships. How many
of us can list families torn apart by a parent so
absorbed with work that he lost his family? These

are usually very insecure people, whose motives are to provide for their families. The Christmas tree is surrounded by expensive presents, but love is missing. Jesus demonstrates that the poor are thankful for consideration. It is not taken for granted or forgotten.

Finally, selfless giving feels the best. Here, Jesus, and later, James, points out that pure (perfect) religion is to visit orphans and widows, in their distress (James 1:27). Why is this pure religion? It is selfless. A widow and an orphan cannot repay. It is truly giving without an expectation of repayment.

What are New Agers doing for the poor? By asking that question, I must be fair and also ask, what is the church doing for the poor, widows and orphans? Jesus is our example.

Forgiveness

Luke 15:1-32:

> Another time, the tax-collectors and sinners were all crowding in to listen to him; and the Pharisees and scribes began murmuring their disapproval: "This fellow," they said, "welcomes sinners and eats with them."

> He answered them with this parable: "If one of you has a hundred sheep and loses one of them, does he not leave the ninety-nine in the wilderness and go after the one that is missing until he finds it? And when he does, he lifts it joyfully on to his shoulders, and goes home to call his friends and neighbors together. 'Rejoice with me!' he cries. 'I have found my lost sheep.' In the same way, I tell you, there will be greater joy in heaven over

one sinner who repents than over ninety-nine righteous people who do not need to repent.

"Or again, if a woman has ten silver coins and loses one of them, does she not light the lamp, sweep out the house, and look in every corner till she finds it? And when she does, she calls her friends and neighbors together, and says, 'Rejoice with me! I have found the coin that I lost.' In the same way, I tell you, there is joy among the angels of God over one sinner who repents."

Again he said: "There was once a man who had two sons; and the younger said to his father, 'Father, give me my share of the property.' So he divided his estate between them. A few days later the younger son turned the whole of his share into cash and left home for a distant country, where he squandered it in dissolute living. He had spent it all, when a severe famine fell upon that country and he began to be in need. So he went and attached himself to one of the local land-owners, who sent him on to his farm to mind the pigs. He would have been glad to fill his belly with the pods that the pigs were eating, but no one gave him anything. Then he came to his senses: 'How many of my father's hired servants have more food than they can eat,' he said, 'and here am I, starving to death! I will go at once to my father's, and say to him, "Father, I have sinned against God and against you; I am no longer fit to be called your son; treat me as one of your hired servants,"' So he set out for his father's house. But while he was still a long way off his father saw him, and his heart went out to him; he ran to meet him, flung his arms around him, and kissed him. The

son said, 'Father, I have sinned against God
and against you; I am no longer fit to be
called your son.' But the father said to his
servants, 'Quick! Fetch a robe, the best we
have, and put it on him; put a ring on his
finger and sandals on his feet. Bring the fatted calf and kill it, and let us celebrate with a
feast. For this son of mine was dead and has
come back to life; he was lost and is found.'
And the festivities began.

Now the elder son had been out on the farm;
and on his way back, as he approached the
house, he heard music and dancing. He called
one of the servants and asked what it meant.
The servant told him, 'Your brother has come
home, and your father has killed the fatted
calf because he has him back safe and sound.]
But he was angry and refused to go in. His
father came out and pleaded with him; but he
retorted, 'You know how I have slaved for
you all these years; I never once disobeyed
your orders; yet you never gave me so much
as a kid, to celebrate with my friends. But
now that this son of yours turns up, after
running through your money with his women,
you kill the fatted calf for him.' 'My boy,' said
the father, 'you are always with me, and everything I have is yours. How could we fail to
celebrate this happy day? Your brother here
was dead and has come back to life; he was
lost and has been found.'"

Love and forgiveness cannot be separated.
As humans we will disappoint our friends and
loved ones, but Jesus gave us the hope and the
command to be reconciled. This is one of the
most misunderstood passages of Scripture. Normally, it is taught as consisting of three separate

parables: the lost coin, the lost sheep, and the lost son. If we examine the context closely, Jesus is teaching a far more significant lesson.

In the first two passages it is clear that Jesus is addressing a group of Pharisees. They were upset because Jesus was talking with tax-gatherers and sinners. At the time of Jesus, tax-gatherers were considered by the Jews to be traitors. The Roman Emperor took bids for those who wished to collect taxes in a given geographical area. In time, the collector would receive a commission on taxes collected. Jews were adverse to paying Rome, particularly through a Jewish collector. And so, the Pharisees are angered by Jesus' choice of friends.

He then offers the lesson of acceptance and forgiveness and unity by using this single parable with three parts. Notice that in the lost coin parable and the lost sheep parable, the expected response of neighbors is *joy* when that which was lost was found. In the extended section, that of the lost or prodigal son, the response of the older brother is the focus. He shows no joy. The point of this three-part parable is to show that the Pharisees should display joy that God is reaching those outside their specific religious community. Let us not lose sight of the overriding message of forgiveness.

In the Prodigal Son, we see a father waiting for a rebellious son. He spotted him while he was yet a far way off. He expected him. There is little doubt that the father in this story represents God. This being so, it is the only time in Scripture that God is presented as being in a hurry: "But while he was still a long way off, his father saw him and felt compassion for him and *ran* and embraced him, and kissed him" (Luke 15:20).

God in a hurry to receive a repentant sinner!
Jesus taught this as the most necessary of all needs.

Matthew 18:21-35:

> Then Peter came to him and asked, "Lord,
> how often am I to forgive my brother if he
> goes on wronging me? As many as seven
> times?"
>
> Jesus replied, "I do not say seven times but
> seventy times seven. The kingdom of Heaven,
> therefore, should be thought of in this way:
> There was once a king who decided to settle
> accounts with the men who served him. At
> the outset, there appeared before him a man
> who owed ten thousand talents. Since he had
> no means of paying, his master ordered him
> to be sold, with his wife, his children, and
> everything he had, to meet the debt.
>
> "The man fell at his master's feet. 'Be patient
> with me,' he implored, 'and I will pay you in
> full'; and the master was so moved with pity
> that he let the man go and canceled the debt.
> But no sooner had the man gone out than he
> met a fellow-servant who owed him a hun-
> dred denarii; he took hold of him, seizing
> him by the throat, and said, 'Pay me what you
> owe.' The man fell at his fellow-servant's feet,
> and begged him, 'Be patient with me, and I
> will pay you'; but he refused, and had him
> thrown into jail until he should pay the debt.
>
> The other servants were deeply distressed
> when they saw what had happened, and they
> went to their master and told him the whole
> story. Then he sent for the man and said,
> 'You scoundrel! I canceled the whole of your

debt when you appealed to me; ought you
not to have shown mercy, too?' And so angry
was the master that he condemned the man
to be tortured until he should pay the debt in
full. That is how my heavenly Father will deal
with you, unless you each forgive your brother
from your hearts."

It has been said that many now held in psychi-
atric institutions could be released if only they
could feel forgiveness. Without this element of
nature, we cannot be social creatures. God intended community. He created man and woman
and commanded then to be fruitful and multiply.
The Jews were a tight-knit nation, and the church
is referred to frequently as a family. We are social
creatures. To survive together, forgiveness is critical. We live in a world that is made up of individuals who want to be forgiven, but are not as likely to
forgive others.

Peter confronts Jesus with this basic human
question, "Lord, How often shall my brother sin
against me and I forgive him? Up to seven times?"
(Luke 18:21). Perhaps Peter's question was not as
sincere as it originally sounds. Peter, as a Jew,
knew that the traditional custom was to forgive
three times. Peter doubles the figure and adds
one. Was this meant to impress Jesus with his
great willingness to forgive and show compassion?
Jesus responds by saying we are to forgive seven
times seventy. Does He literally mean four hundred and ninety times. No! The point is that we
are to continue to forgive, again and again.

Jesus goes on to share a parable of human
nature and forgiveness. Jesus does know the human mind, and here he demonstrates it. How easy

it is to see only with tunnel vision—to see only beyond our own needs. Compassion is the key. Jesus knows the hearts of all men and sees their greatest need.

If the New Age acknowledges no sin, then there is no need for fogivness. We have yet to see the emotional trauma to be suffered by New Agers.

Jesus is my example. The principles He espoused are certainly humanitarian. He demonstrated their practicality. And finally, He showed that they are not compatible with a New Age philosophy. One might say, "Sure, Jesus could live this type of life, but I'm a 'regular walking around type guy.' It's impossible for me to act this humanely. The value system He taught worked for Him, but not today."

The answer to this is not complicated. Jesus faced, as we've demonstrated, the same issues that we face today. Can you and I do it? Can we carry on the morality taught by Jesus? Listen to His words from John 14:15: "If you love me, you will keep my commandments."

And in Matthew 28:19,20: "Go therefore and make disciples of *all the nations*, baptizing them in the name of the Father and the Son and the Holy Spirit, teaching them to *observe all that I commanded* you; and lo, I am with you always, even to the end of the age."

A major distinction between Christianity and the New Age is that we are never alone. Not only has Jesus promised to be with us always, but He also promised the indwelling of His Holy Spirit to guide us into all righteousness (Acts 2:38). Would He command us to do something that He knew would be impossible?

Jesus teaches us that great spiritual leaders

are first great followers of Him. The gods of the New Age fall far short in word and example. All the great avatars of the past are buried; with the exception of one, the tombs are marked "Occupied."

NINE

The Family as Partners in Education

When something goes wrong, it is important to talk, not about who is to blame, but about who is going to fix it.

In 1986 the Wisconsin Association of School Board Delegates' general assembly approved a resolution entitled "Parent-School Partnerships Are Necessary for Effective Schools." The resolution read: "The WASB urges each school board to establish policies on parent involvement (individual and group) and to encourage their active participation in the educational process through scheduled events, increased teacher-parent communications, and parent education programs."[1]

As this group noted, research studies show that parental involvement is essential in creating effective schools. Across the country, education groups, commissions, and teachers are encouraging parental involvement. Specific programs like "Parents as Teachers" are reinforcing the idea of parents working closely with the schools.

For many parents, active involvement has been

a way of life. From the PTO volunteer to the library helper and the chief car-pool driver, moms everywhere have paid the price. But, today we need to have *both* parents involved in the schools. Not just in the day-to-day routines, but in the "nuts and bolts" of the school curriculum.

Organizing a Parent Group

Many parents want to become partners in education, but they don't know where to begin. They have concerns about curriculum, textbooks, or activities, but don't know where or how to express their concerns.

Ann Fahrenkrug, of Larson, Wisconsin, started a parenting network in her community. Her primary purpose for forming the group was to provide parents an opportunity to communicate with other parents about their concerns.

Your concern may be global education or New Age themes in textbooks. Whatever the concern, organizing a parent group is the beginning of getting your message heard. That is how the Smiths got started.

Mike and Jane Smith were tired of going it alone. They had been fighting with the school district for years, trying to educate them on the New Age themes in the curriculum. But they weren't taken seriously. So they decided to change their approach. They would involve other parents.

Mike decided to write a letter to all the parents at his son's school. His one-page, xeroxed letter was informational, explaining why the parent group was needed. It listed the time, place, date, and agenda of the meeting. At the bottom of the letter was a tear-off for attending the meeting.

The day of the meeting, Mike called the hotel to confirm the time and room. Mike knew the room atmosphere was important, so he arrived an hour early to set up. He placed his flip charts in view and focused the overhead projector before anyone arrived. His name, address, and phone number were in large letters on the blackboard. The group's name was laminated and taped to the wall.

He knew most people had not heard of New Age terminology, so he xeroxed a vocabulary list to hand out. On tables next to the door, he had New Age terms and phrases highlighted in photocopies of textbooks, curriculum guides, and activity sheets. Mike knew he could not just talk about an issue. He had to show people *why* he was concerned.

At seven o'clock sharp, he started the meeting. With this type of format, Mike was able to recruit enough people to start a parent group. You can, too, if you follow a few simple guidelines:

1. Set the meeting date at least eight weeks before the meeting and send out reminder notices or call individual parents;

2. Have a one- or two-page sheet describing the issues that will be discussed sent to all the people;

3. Choose a meeting place that is centrally located and easily accessible;

4. Decide what type of format the meeting should follow: formal, panel, workshop, or lecture; it's best to have a formal meeting first, and as the group progresses, to switch to other formats;

5. Have handouts, because people want something they can take with them; volunteer sheets;

summaries of a school history; and issue updates can be placed in a small folder and handed out at the beginning of the meeting.

The Meeting

1. Start on time and end on time; people have other obligations;

2. Use an agenda and stick to it; cover all the points; additional concerns are for the next meeting;

3. Have people fill out volunteer sheets;

4. Provide for question and answer time;

5. Schedule a follow-up meeting; ask members what day and time is best.

After the Meeting

1. Send notices to all the members, thanking them for attending; thank them for volunteering their time to improve their schools;

2. Two weeks before the scheduled meeting, send out reminder notices to all members;

3. Prepare a newsletter to keep members informed and excited about what is happening;

4. Before the second meeting, have the officers of the group set up volunteer committees; inform the committee members of their assignments before the meeting.

Make-Up of a Parent Group

An effective parent group usually has a chairperson, vice-chairperson, recording secretary, corresponding secretary, and treasurer.

The chairperson functions as the spokesperson for the group and prepares all the agendas. The vice-chairperson assumes the role of the chairman in case of absence and plays the host role at local meetings. The recording secretary gives the typed, xeroxed minutes to the corresponding secretary to send to members. The treasurer handles the funds.

The committees for the group vary according to need. A fully functioning parent group could have a membership, school, research, issues, legislative, school board, and leadership training committee.

The membership committee formulates a plan to recruit members, parents and non-parents. Since 70 percent of the people in a community do not have children in school, the committee designs a systematic plan to involve non-parents. They develop goals and objectives for the year and report back to the group. The school committee is the bridge between parents and teachers. Through their effective personal communication with teachers, they construct a permanent bridge of trust and openness. They do this by

· holding one-on-one conferences;
· supporting teachers in good time and bad;
· hosting a coffee or "welcome back" in the fall;
· holding an educational forum;
· encouraging, listening, and working positively;
· developing an attitude of mutual cooperation.

This non-threatening approach enables them to reach teachers on issues that affect children. As one committee member stated, "The key to working with teachers is building a trusting relationship, a relationship built on 'respect.'"

The research and issues committees work together, gathering information from various sources. Conservative groups, publishers, libraries, and state education associations provide current data on issues. The committee provides one-page issue statements to the other committee members who lobby for the group.

The legislative committee keeps abreast of state issues. After writing or visiting an elected official, they publish the legislative update to members and teachers. They do this on a regular basis so teachers receive both sides of an issue.

The leadership training committee organizes workshops for members in certain areas, such as how to implement a meeting working with school officials, and letter-writing campaigns addressing legislators. The committee surveys its members on the type of workshop it needs and fulfills the need. A morning workshop is usually held in the fall with twenty to twenty-five members participating.

The school board committee builds relationships with its board members. They do this through one-on-one visits at a breakfast, lunch, or dinner. The goal is to get to know them on a personal basis and then to become a resource to them. They provide key literature on issues or direct them to sources for information. They attend board meetings and lobby individual members. Their key is to speak politely, without emotion, and in a non-threatening way.

As Christians, we have a responsibility to be involved with our school boards. As Abraham Lincoln said, "Today's classrooms are tomorrow's government."

Parent Groups in Action

How would you react to an "elementary guidance program" that taught concepts contrary to Christian values, or school programs that emphasized "self," and taught through "guided fantasy" or "role playing"? Two Wisconsin couples responded by forming a parent group called People for Basic Education. "Their values," speaking of the school's, "were not our values," said the group. So they pulled their children from public schools, enrolled them in Christian schools, and began a crusade to change the public schools through People for Basic Education.

The group focused on analyzing student programs and teaching strategies, then informing parents, school administrators, and school board members of their findings. Their seventeen-page critical analysis of the "elementary guidance program" presented facts on both sides of the issues. Their professional manner when presenting the analysis won favor with many in the audience.

Analyses of the programs or teaching strategies of one-to-three pages are the norm for many groups. The group didn't stop with analyzing programs. They prepared policy statements and guidelines and distributed them to members, administrators, teachers, and concerned citizens. One policy statement looked like this:

We, the People for Basic Education,

1. believe, after reviewing instructional materials for such programs as guidance, personal development, moral education, values clarifications, and citizenship programs, and other classroom strategies utilized in some aspects of Public privacy of child, parent and family; undermine parental authority; portray parents in a negative light; and fail to inform children of fixed moral standard of right and wrong, but instead tell the child he is free to

create his own right and wrong moral values
based on a philosophy of ever-changing situations (without any express reference to the
fixed standards and authority of parents,
creed, religion or law);

2. believe that social workers, psychologists,
counselors, and specialized student assistance
and social service type programs can play an
important role in helping those particular
high-risk problems but that this should and
must be done outside the regular classroom
and either in one-to-one counseling or in special small groups and special programs; this is
essential not only to protect the privacy and
the feelings of those children with problems
but also in order to respect the family privacy
and valuable class time of those non-partici-
pating children who deserve to receive the
maximum amount of academic instruction
time;

3. believe that respect for the value and integrity of the family requires that any guidance,
counseling, psychological or other "personal
assessment" services provided to a child should
only occur after fully informed parental consent is obtained;

4. believe that questionnaires, personal inven-
tories, diaries, journals, or hand-out sheets
that require the child (who is, after all, a
"captive audience") to reveal personal and
private emotions or attitudes, or that probe
into psychological aspects of the child's personality or personal, moral, or family values,
violate the privacy and integrity of the child
and parent alike;

5. believe that discussions, role playing games,
or "moral dilemma" exercises that present

school children with difficult, open-ended
moral questions without giving absolute moral
answers or definite ethical rules are an exercise in social and educational chaos because
psychologists have stated that grade school
children in general lack the cognitive development to meaningfully handle hypothetical,
"what if" or "choices and consequences" type
questions.[2]

This is but part of one of their policy statements. Another handout provided is "Guidelines
for Evaluating Any Classroom Material," which
includes information such as:

Do questions ask children to disclose feelings
or opinions about themselves, friends, or family members?

Do questions ask your child to express what
makes him afraid, anxious, uncomfortable,
sad, depressed, happy, or secure?

Do questions portray parents as non-caring,
abusive, alcoholic, old-fashioned, unable to
meet a child's needs?

Do questions ask your child to rank, rate,
compare, evaluate, criticize, or question his
values or those of his family or his religion?

Do questions portray your child in a negative
light? (poor self-esteem, drug or alcohol problems).

Do they ask open-ended moral dilemma or
role playing questions?[3]

With handouts like this, it is no wonder this
group was so successful in working with the public
schools.

You can be successful, too, by adapting some of the procedures presented in this chapter to your situation. You will see your school grow in moral content.

Prayer and Action

We are all concerned for our schools and for the children in them. The hour is late, and our schools are in a state of crisis. But by working together, we can make a difference. If you can't get physically involved, then please pray. Start a "Moms in Touch" program in your city. Have people pray daily for our children and schools.

The columnist, Cal Thomas, feels this way about prayer: "The reason the distance between our feet and knees is short is because after we get up off our knees from praying, we should put our feet to use and do something."

Today, won't you get involved in helping our public schools become the storehouse of opportunity that our forefathers once knew?

TEN

Organize to Educate

"Today's classrooms are tomorrow's government"–

Abraham Lincoln

Not only do we need an active parent group to fight the spread of "New Age" education in the schools, we also need an informed "education group" within the church—a group that instructs, mobilizes, and informs members on current issues that effect our children.

When organizing an "education group," remember that you are trying to educate people on the issues. The "education group" could be part of the Sunday school, home fellowship, Bible studies, or Sunday night services. Once the group has become informed and mobilized, it can join with other coalitions in the city to fight the same issues. Here is a story of how two women kept their church informed.

Jane, a working mom with two children, and Sue, a homemaker, decided to combine their talents, energy, and wisdom. Both women were concerned with the direction of public schools and wanted to do something. Since Jane was a secretary, she knew how to organize, obtain, and disseminate information; she would handle all the clerical work. Sue's artistic talents and public speaking abilities made her a perfect choice for designing displays and speaking out on the issues. Before they got started, they went to their pastor and presented him with the idea. He liked it and presented it to the church board, which overwhelmingly approved. Within a month, Jane and Sue were on their way to a successful program.

They started out by constructing a small bulletin board. On it, they displayed current educational issues, letters to the editor, letters to representatives, and notice of school events. From this, parents were encouraged to write and express their opinions. Not only did parents write, but the education classes helped them learn how to speak out on the issues.

Within the Church

Jane and Sue's program met the needs of their church. There are many ways to organize an "education group" within your church. The program design that you implement will fit your church personality, needs, and goals. As the format evolved, the successful ingredients will be: an executive committee, coordinator of concerns, secretary, legislative coordinator, newsletter coordinator, educational coordinator, and public relations coordinator.

The executive committee is responsible for implementing, designing, and promoting the program. The size of the group will depend on the size of your church. A church of two hundred might have a six-member committee. Members should be chosen with care; consider their talents, interests, knowledge, and enthusiasm. A one-year commitment, monthly meetings, and weekly assignments are not unusual for this type of committee.

The coordinator of concerns is responsible for overseeing the entire operation. He will discuss and inform the pastor and deacons on events, issues, and executive meetings. (When meeting with a pastor, make an appointment and give him a copy of the agenda before you meet.) The coordinator will lead the monthly meeting and provide the pastor with a written summary. He will keep abreast of the issues and be the principle spokesperson for the group. He will be responsible for coordinating a yearly program for the congregation and attend and assist all the educational meetings.

The secretary is responsible to the chairman. He will record and distribute the minutes to the committee, pastor and board; and post it on the bulletin board. He will notify members of scheduled meetings and will handle all the correspondence for the group.

The legislative coordinator is the arm between the legislature and the church. He receives his information through newsletters and visits with his representative. He informs the coordinator and committee of the impending educational bills that are of interest to the church. He is the principle spokesperson for contacting our representatives and obtaining updates on current issues. Upon consent of the pastor and board, he will address the church body regarding specific issues. The coordinator will prepare a legislative scoreboard for local, state, and national races.

The newsletter coordinator is a person who enjoys writing, who can meet deadlines and be able to coordinate his responsibilities with two or more people. He is responsible for teaching the congregation how to write an effective letter to the editor. He will design and implement an "Effective Citizen" brochure and will publish a monthly newsletter.

The public relations coordinator is responsible for teaching current educational issues and citizenship in a home fellowship setting. He trains new people every fall and addresses the church, when needed.

Volunteers

The volunteer rate in the United States is decreasing, because we are not asking for help. More people would become involved today, if they were asked. Below are some suggestions on developing an effective volunteer force.

1. Treat your volunteers with respect;
2. Make them feel welcome, useful, needed and appreciated;
3. Show them that their job is important to the big picture;
4. Give specific assignments and thorough instructions;
5. Give assignments they can complete;
6. Help make the working conditions pleasant;
7. Be patient and smile frequently;

8. Thank them. (You cannot thank volunteers enough.)

No group can function without volunteers—people who dedicate their time and talents to making an organization work, who willingly perform services without pay. They are the glue that holds it all together. We say, "I need your help," and people from all walks of life come forth to lend a helping hand. Just think what would happen in the church if all the pew sitters became active. The liberal media wouldn't know how to handle it.

How to Network the Issues

Not only is it important to inform and educate your members on educational issues, you must reach the busy church people and the people beyond the church doors. You are not going to personally touch base with everyone, but, indirectly, you can reach many through a variety of methods.

Information Center

One way to network the issues is through an information center. The center could be located where a large number of people would pass and be able to stop to view the information. A large professional tag-board display with current educational issue updates, hand-outs, newsletters and information brochures, city news, representatives' letters, names, addresses and phone numbers of committee members, and the agendas for weekly activities could be posted. Under the bulletin board could be a small table for literature, citizen brochures, library check-out, and issues updates. A suggestion box and 4 x 6 enrollment cards would be located in the center of the table.

Elected Official

Ask the elected official to present his stand on the educational issues to your education group. Then, invite the congregation to ask questions. To help the program run smoothly, prepare a sample list of questions ahead of time and present it to the candidate before the session. Also, prepare a candidate position paper and distribute it to the congregation before the program.

Brochure

A third way to inform members is through a brochure. They are inexpensive to prepare and easy to distribute. The basic content describes the goals and objectives of the group and will enable more people to become involved and not feel threatened.

Suggestions for construction:

1. What to put in the brochure:

    a. Give reasons for Christians to be involved in an education group;

    b. Cite the biblical base for Christian responsibility;

    c. Define the meaning of separation of church and state;

    d. Define the purpose and goals of the group;

    e. Give examples of how they can get involved.

2. What to put on the back of the brochure:

    a. The officers' names, telephone numbers, and addresses;

   b. Whom to contact for more information;

   c. Time and place of meetings.

3. How to construct the brochure:

   a. It's a good idea to have two different colors (black and white) for background and a bold color for words you want highlighted. This adds contrast and draws the reader in.

   b. Try not to clutter with too much copy.

   c. A two- or three-fold brochure works well. Good color and photos are essential.

   d. All the graphics must have a purpose and a goal. Coordinate the graphics with the theme. Remember the graphics are the first contact a person has with your group. It is important.

   e. The price depends on the amount of type setting, photos, and art work. Try to find a church member willing to volunteer his talents for constructing this. The cost ranges from $24 to $40 for constructing it, without printing costs.

Weekly Newsletter

The fourth communication tool is a weekly newsletter. This can be used as a public relations tool to inspire new members and be informative; it features the latest news and issues updates.

Preparing a newsletter is simple. If your church owns a computer, there are many fine computer software packages that specialize in newsletter writing. Or, you can use the conventional cut and paste method to construct it. Whatever method you use, it's best to have committees with specific positions to ensure a smooth running program—news editor, copy editor, typesetter, researcher, etc.

Before you begin, select a committee and a news editor. The editor handles the entire production (layout, content, distribution). Choose someone from your church who has experience in news reporting or English. Select a staff that can assist in typing, designing, proofreading, collating, and distributing. The key is to find people who are enthused about the job.

The content centers around the goals and objectives of the group. A suggested format might be:

Article 1: Message from the coordinator's desk;

Article 2: Legislative update on education;

Article 3: Issues updates on local education;

Article 4: Weekly agenda;

Article 5: Citizens response (comments and concerns from the congregation);

Article 6: Schedule of upcoming events.

Because of our fast-paced society, Christians do not have the time to dig for answers. This might be their only source of accurate information on legislative and community educational concerns. That is why it is so important to be accurate and concise in reporting. Give only the facts; stay away from opinions and emotions as much as possible. Consider this activity to be another form of motivating people to action.

Essentials for Construction of a Weekly Newsletter

1. Do not crowd the page. Make it attractive and readable.

2. Use headlines, graphs, and pictures appropriately.

3. Use a new ribbon for clear, dark print.

4. Headlines and pictures are available at an office supply store.

5. Leave 1 inch margins on top, 3/4 inch margins on the bottom, and 1/2 inch margins on the side.

6. Keep reading material at the sixth grade level. Be readable. Use short, simple sentences—not over twenty words. Keep paragraphs under seven lines in length. Indent all paragraphs five spaces.

7. Choose a format and color scheme and stick to it.

8. Get the reader's attention in the first story. Arouse his interest so he will read the rest of the newsletter.

9. Present the facts to the readers—avoid condemnation.

10. Make it friendly, interesting, and keep it moving.

11. Keep in mind: you want to move the Christian from inaction to action.

There are eight important points to keep in mind when communicating with others.

1. Get people to hear your message.

• Be attuned to your audience. What is their educational, cultural, and economic level? If you are speaking to a rural farming group, don't walk in wearing a three-piece suit, using statistics that don't pertain to them.

• State the facts and stay away from opinions. People are smart enough to know the difference.

- Present yourself as the authority. Know your topic inside and out.

- Be confident. Believe in what you are saying and doing.

- Display good body language. Look directly in your audience's eyes when speaking. Don't look away or be distracted; it will be perceived that you don't care about what you're saying. Be calm and speak slowly and concisely.

- Wear subdued clothing and jewelry. You want people to focus on what you say.

- State a purpose for them to listen to you. Begin your speech with a good lead and then provide sequential steps to support your lead.

- Be positive.

2. *How to deal with negative people*
a. The Non-Christian

1. Restate the negative comment into one that is positive.

2. Explain to the person that in every situation, you try to find the positive.

3. Don't argue with him, but silently say a prayer that God will change his attitude.

4. If the situation is right, encourage him to pray and fellowship with Bible-believing people.

b. The Bible-believing Christian

1. Seek forgiveness and restoration.

2. Show him Scripture passages that point to controlling our thought life.

3. How to change the mind of the community

a. Vote. Every person's vote is important. You can decide the city council race, mayoral race, state senate race, or presidential race. The decision made in the voting booth can change the mind of government in your community and nation.

b. Get involved in a political party. Here, you can recruit, nominate, and elect members to public office. You will be with people who share the same ideas and goals for government who can work together to persuade voters to vote for your candidate.

c. Join a special interest group. These people share common goals and objectives and seek to influence public groups and elected officials.

d. Write letters. Letters-to-the-editor are read by many people in the community and are an excellent source for changing people's opinions.

4. How to respond with the facts

First, state the facts in a slow, sequential manner and end with a short summary.

When called upon in an interview, press conference, or informal gathering, reiterate the facts that have been verified as accurate. Stay away from expressing your own opinion, and people will be more inclined to listen to what you have to say.

5. *How to deal with criticism*

Criticism by a colleague or another volunteer may be directed at you, but the problem lies not with you, but the attacker. How do you handle unnecessary verbal abuse?

Begin by looking at the attacker. Ask yourself: What is he really saying? What is his perception of me? Of this campaign?

There are two ways to approach problems:

a. Take a friend and visit this person. Explain what you have heard, and that you would like to end the gossip right now. Present the facts and seek a reconciliation.

b. When involved in another event with the person, try to encourage and praise the person for her efforts. Show her that you believe she is a worthwhile individual through your positive actions.

c. Above all, include this person in your daily prayer life. Seek the will of God for her and lift her up daily for the love of God that she is searching for.

6. *How to speak in public*

If you feel uneasy or self-conscious about speaking in public, consider taking a professional speaking course. I know I benefited from Toastmasters International, a public speaking group for men and women. I learned the basic techniques of body language, speech delivery, and much more. Listed below are some of the techniques I would like to share with you:

a. Speak loudly and clearly so the audience in the back can hear you. Don't always speak in the same tone of voice; vary your tone.

b. Look directly at your audience. Good eye contact is a must. Try to find one or two people to focus on. If you can't look them in the eyes, focus on their hair line.

c. Begin your speech by clarifying your purpose. Why are you speaking to them?

d. Give them only the information they need to form an opinion.

e. Organize your speech in a sequential manner. Show the pros and cons of the subject matter. Provide the facts to support your major details. End your speech by summarizing the main ideas.

When I give a public speech, I write the main ideas and details on 3 x 5 cards. I underline the first word in every sentence in red so I will not lose my place while I am speaking. Another technique is to use visuals. Present them during the speech to draw interest and help people remember what you are saying.

Practice! You can never be over-prepared. Read your speech in front of a mirror with a tape recorder going and play it back to see how you are progressing. If you can have someone video tape your speech and then give a constructive critique, you will benefit greatly.

7. *How to approach someone with a concern*

a. THROUGH LOVE, be willing to risk and

to follow through with your concern. Risk
going beyond your comfort zone, but stay
within the realm of love when confronting.

b. <u>DON'T</u> accuse or be demanding. Present
the facts to the person in a neutral setting.
Allow the person time to think about what
you have said and to clear his mind of any
false accusations he may have.

c. <u>DON'T</u> be a "Know-it-All." There are two
sides to an issue. Preview the issue with an
open mind and collectively try to decide the
issue at hand from the facts.

Through active involvement, we can put the
educational system back together. Begin your involvement today. Be an innovator, create a system
within your church that will work through the
educational system in our society.

Authors' Call to Action

Dr. George Twente, a psychiatrist in Alabama
alarmed at the New Age concepts taught in the
public schools, said this in a recent article for
Citizens for Excellence in Education:

> It is my opinion that if most of these teachers
> and especially parents of the children knew
> the origin of these techniques and the poten-
> tial for emotional, mental and spiritual ma-
> nipulation, they would not teach, encourage
> or allow their children to participate. I fur-
> ther encourage school officials to get informed
> consent from the parents for these psycho-
> logical and/or religious techniques to be used
> and then only by trained, accredited profes-
> sionals.[1]

Dr. Twente is right that if teachers and parents knew what the "New Age" was all about, they wouldn't allow it to be taught in the public schools. Our job then is to inform them. We have a duty as Christian citizens to inform and be informed, to do our part to bring Christian values to the shaping of public policy, and to go out and actively oppose that which is wrong. Through obedience, commitment, knowledge, and action, we can change our Public Schools to be the educational institutions they once were.

School Boards

Did you know that everything is set in a school board meeting: standards, curriculum, budget, hiring and firing. And did you know that your school board reflects the attitude of your community? They set the moral and spiritual tone. Now you might be asking, "How does this happen?" First, the school board hires the superintendent, who hires the principals, who in turn hire the teachers. Now if that superintendent has the same view as the community, we're okay. But if his world view is that of a special interest group then more than likely so are the teachers and principals that he hires. That can be a problem. As you can see, the superintendent is a key player, and it is worth your while to get to know him and to build a strong relationship with him.

Meetings

Where do you begin? Begin by attending a school board meeting. If you don't know where or when they are held, call the school district's board office, or the superintendent's office. They can tell you the time, place, agenda, who the board members are, their addresses, and phone numbers.

Before you attend a meeting, I would suggest you go to your local public library and check out a book on school boards. You will be a much better player if you know how the system works. Study and memorize the book, *Robert's Rules of Order*. Learn how to table a motion, second a motion, or close a meeting. This book is invaluable for people who want to have their opinion heard and make a difference.

Next, find out everything you can on the board members. Who are they? How long have they served? What is their background? When are their terms over? What are the qualifications for a board member? This background information will allow you to look like a professional and zero in faster on your objective for being there.

At the first meeting, go with the intent of learning how the system works. Who are the key people? What is being discussed? Who are the power people? How many people attend? What week do they meet? How often do they meet? What committees can you attend? After the meeting, personally introduce yourself to the board. Go up to the board members after the meeting and politely say "Hello, Mrs. Jones, my name is Barb Smith. I am a parent and interested in our schools." Always smile and have direct eye contact. When concluding your short introduction, use the person's name in ending the conversation. This personalizes the conversation and shows her that you are trying to get to know her.

Remember you do not have to know all the board members the first night, nor do you have to know everything about the school board process the first night. You are there for the long haul. It took time for them to learn the process, and it will take you time to learn it also. Don't become anxious. Take it one step at a time. Keep in mind that you are trying to build relationships, and relationships are not built overnight.

While attending board meetings, take notes. Write down what is being said and not said. Keep a file of all the handouts and any newspaper clippings pertaining to school news. This can be used as research, teaching, or future debate material.

To gain the respect of board members, visitors, and participants, dress and act like you are attending an important meeting. Arrive early with clipboard and pencil in hand and sit near the front so you can avoid any talkers during the meeting.

Research the Issues

In order to speak out on the issues, you need to do your homework. How do you get the facts? First, check your Bible. What is it saying about the issue? Ask your pastor his views. Check with your Bible study group, maybe they have studied the issues in class. Then ask yourself, how does this issue affect me, my community, or my nation? What is the aim of this issue? Where is it headed?

If it is a new curriculum, call your state department of public instruction, public library, school district curriculum director, or a Christian group that is "up" on the issue and can give you the latest statistics. The bottom line is you need to research your subject well before you can address it before a group. You want to know both sides of the issue so you can debate it effectively.

After you feel comfortable with a couple of key issues, focus your time on developing a relationship with one school board member. Get to know him or her on a personal level. Take him or her out for breakfast or lunch. At the first get-together be informal; developing a trusting relationship is more important than debating the issues. As your relationship builds, be a resource to him or her. Provide him or her with literature on key issues or direct him or her to various sources for information. Remember other special interest groups are out there doing this. And if the board member doesn't get the information from you, it will come from the other side.

Let's say that after a year of attending school board meetings you become upset with the new curriculum that is laced with "New Age" material, about to be adopted at the next board meeting. You studied the issue and are prepared to speak out at the next board meeting. Before you step forward at the meeting with your concerns, take these concerns to each board member. Individually lobby each board member before the meeting. It would do you no good to go in with all the factual information and expect every board member to change his or her vote. Remember: a school board member is a volunteer with another job and possibly a family. He receives stacks of material that he doesn't have time to read and generally lets the superintendent do all the research. That is why it is so important to lobby the individual members before the meeting. Do it politely—without emotion. Present yourself on a non-threatening level, and you will be successful.

Lobbying

Follow these eight lobbying steps and see how you can make a difference. When approaching school personnel or a school board member:

1. Know the opposition: Find out what the teacher's union, curriculum director, or superintendent is saying about the new curriculum. Who are the key players in the schools for, or against, the curriculum? In the community? Who are the publishers of the curriculum? Who reviewed the curriculum?

2. Know the issue: What does your opponent have to say about it? What does the latest research say? Why are you against it? Why are you for it? Can you discuss it without becoming emotional? Can you present the facts in a sequential manner?

3. Follow through on each point of contact: If you contact a school board member personally, follow it up with a written letter thanking him for the meeting. If you see a school board member downtown and casually talk to him about an issue, follow it up with a written note expressing your appreciation.

4. Be accurate: Check your facts carefully. People will remember your mistakes.

5. Work with coalitions: If you are working on a school board issue, check to see what other groups in the community are doing. Work together if possible. Check with national conservative groups like Concerned Women for America. Maybe someone else from around the country is experiencing the same problem, and you could pick up some ideas on how to approach the problem from them.

6. Study the process: Do a complete research at the library. Know the steps of a school board meeting and how to get your concern across to a group.

7. Be committed: Don't give up on your cause. Remember, when you are standing up for what is right, you will receive opposition.

8. Avoid attacks: Attack the issue not the person.

Prayer and Action

Remember the prophet Daniel? How did he gain the respect of men and kings? How did he work in a society that was adverse to his thinking? Daniel was famous for two things: prudence and prayer. As a prince, he had power with God and men; by prayer, he had power with God, by prudence, he had power with man, and in both he prevailed. Today we can use Daniel's methods and win. By incorporating these two concepts, prudence and prayer, we can change a situation.

You now know how to effectively lobby and win a school board issue. The next step is to organize prayer groups to pray for every step, every word, every thought that you make as you step forward to fight the "New Age" movement in the schools.

This battle cannot be fought by human flesh alone. We need the strength and support of the many tireless prayer warriors that grace every church in this land. You need to be backed by a prayer team that prays for your:

Vision: A vision that sees the public schools as the store house of knowledge, that includes God, Godly principle, and prayer in its curriculum.

Life: That your life will be a witness to the many people you touch and that they may be brought to know Jesus as their Lord and Savior.

Schools: That each school, school board member, school personnel, and student are prayed for daily for the protection against the "New Age" movement.

Spiritual Awakening: Pray that our schools and America will receive a new spiritual awakening.

We are concerned for our schools and for the children in America. The hour is late and the situation is desperate. Our schools are in a state of crisis. Won't you please join the authors today and become active in your public schools? By working together, we can again regain the influence that was lost many years ago when Christians began dropping out of the system.

As the Christopher's keep reminding us, "It is better to light one little candle than to curse the darkness."

EPILOGUE

Final Thoughts

The authors of this book in no way intend to establish an adversarial relationship between parents and teachers or school administrators. We are partners with the same goal: to lovingly instruct our children so that they can become all that God intended. Let us keep in mind that to "war" among ourselves is to miss the point and to misdirect our frustration and even anger. Our God is a God not of confusion but of order and truth. It is our desire that together we can join forces and defeat the "author of lies."

APPENDIX ONE

Textbook Publishers

Below is a listing of names and addresses of textbook publishers. Write and request a catalogue for review. Look to see what materials contain New Age themes. Order the materials you think are questionable, study them, and present your findings in a one-page paper to the publisher. Your actions will alert textbook publishers and in-house writers that there are people who care about the content of textbooks.

1. Trillium Press
   P.O. Box 209R
   Monroe, NY 10950

Trillium Press puts out *The Reading Writing Thinking Connection*. Materials contain imagery, guided fantasy, visualization, and graphics of the occult.

2. Scholastic Inc.
   P.O. Box 7501
   2931 East McCarty Street
   Jefferson City, MO 65102

Scholastic publishes the *Whole Language Source Book*.

3. The Wright Group
   19201-120th Ave. NE
   Bothell, WA 98011-9512

The Wright Group publishes *Whole Language* integrated learning resources.

4. American School Publishers
   155 North Wacker Drive
   Chicago, IL 60606

Ask for the *Whole Language* catalogue.

5. Modern Curriculum Press
   A Paramount Communications Company
   13900 Prospect Road
   Cleveland, OH 44136

Modern Curriculum Press publishes *Whole Language*, folklore, interactive fiction, and poetry.

6. Wieser Educational, Inc
   30081 Comercio, Dept. T90
   Rancho Santa Margarita, CA 92688

Wieser is publisher of *Choices and Challenges* program, deals with anti-family stands.

7. Harcourt, Brace, Jovanovich, Inc.
   School Department
   Orlando, FL 32887

Harcourt, Brace, Jovanovich, Inc. publishes the *Impression* series and other *Whole Language* concepts. New Age themes are present in many series.

8. Bks
   Paperback Avenue
   Charlotteville, NY 12036

Bks is a paperback book publisher with books containing New Age concepts.

9. Camelot Avon Flare,
   105 Madison Avenue
   New York, NY 10016

Avon books contain many books with the New Age theme.

10. Curriculum Associates Inc.
    5 Esquire Road
    N. Billerica, MA 01862-2589

Curriculum Associates is a promoter of "self-esteem" and "drug awareness" and "whole language" education programs.

Associations

Listed below are some national and international associations that make educational decisions affecting children. Knowing what the goals and objectives of the associations are will help you keep abreast of current research and programs. By writing the association, you can keep up to date on new curriculum methods, materials, and training seminars. When writing the association, ask for the goals, objectives, and mission statement of the group, along with a membership application form.

For more information on associations, contact your local library. Ask for the *Encyclopedia of Associations* (three volumes, Gale Research Publishers, 1992 edition). To find out more information on the associations listed below, check the number in the *Encyclopedia of Associations* at your local library.

Association for Humanistic Psychology (AHP)
1772 Vallejo, Ste. 3
San Francisco, CA 94123

The AHP is a worldwide network of people who promote humanistic philosophy.

Association for Women in Psychology (AWP)
c/o Angela R. Gillem, Ph.D.
Haverford College
370 Lancaster Ave.
Haverford, PA 19041-1392

The association studies issues of child-rearing practices, lifestyles, language use, and other issues to end sex bias. (Gives Lesbian Psychologies Unpublished Manuscript

Awards annually.)

American Federation of Teachers
555 New Jersey Ave., NW
Washington, DC 20001

The AFT is a teachers' association that represents members' concerns.

National Education Association (NEA)
1201 16th St. NW
Washington, DC 20036

The NEA is the largest teachers' association, representing 2,000,800 members.

Overseas Education Association (OEA)
1201 16th St., NW
Washington, DC 20036

The OEA is a professional association and labor union founded in 1956.

Global Education Associates (International
Understanding) (GEA)
475 Riverside Dr., Ste. 456
New York, NY 10115

The GEA is an association that focuses on promoting a "just world order." (Holds Global workshops.)

National Center for Health Education
(NCHE)
30 E. 29th St., 3rd Fl.
New York, NY 10016

The center develops and provides model programs to schools.

Association For Death Education and Counseling (Thanatology) (ADEC)
636 Prospect Ave.

Hartford, CT 06105

Members upgrade death education materials for schools, churches, hospitals, and other institutions. (Gives workshops and seminars.)

American Association of Sex Educators, Counselors, and Therapists (Sexual Health) (AASECT)
435 N. Michigan Ave., Ste. 1717
Chicago, IL 60611

AASECT is an association that sets competency standards, develops curricula, and trains professionals in the field.

American Forum For Global Education (International Exchange) (AFGE)
45 John St., Ste. 1200
New York, NY

AFGE provides workshops and training seminars to teachers as an insurance that global perspectives are a part of the K-12 curriculum.

Center for Social Studies Education (CSSE)
3857 Willow Ave.
Pittsburgh, PA 15234

The CSSE develops curriculum on critical thinking for secondary and university levels.

Social Science Education Consortium (Social Studies) (SSEC)
33 Mitchell Ln., Ste. 240
Boulder, CA 60301-2272

The SSEC trains educators at all levels on innovative social science education. (Involved in textbooks, multimedia kits, and games.)

Commission on Gay/Lesbian Issues in Social
Work Education
c/o Council on Social Work Educ.
1600 Duke St.
Alexandria, VA 22314

The Commission works to incorporate their philosophy into social work education curriculum.

International Council on Education for
Teaching (Teachers) (ICET)
2009 N. 14th St., Ste. 609
Arlington, VA 22201

The ICET prides itself on serving as the voice of the teachers and provides innovative teaching models.

National Association of State Directors of
Teacher Education and Certification
(Teachers) (NASDTEC)
c/o Dr. Donald Hair
3600 Whitman Ave. N., Ste. 105
Seattle, WA 98103

NASDTEC deals primarily with the preparation and certification of professional personnel, standards, and practices.

Global Learning (International Studies) (GL)
1018 Stuyvesant Ave.
Union, NJ 07083

The GL trains teachers on global concepts. Founded in 1974, it is a non-membership association.

Center For Global Education
(International Understanding) (CGE)
Augsburg College
731-21st Ave. S.
Minneapolis, MN 55454

The CGE seeks to educate on social change and provide educational programs on global issues.

Joint Council on Economic Education
(Economics) (JCEE)
432 Park Ave. S.
New York, NY 10016

A large budget allows for the JCEE's promotion of curriculum development and research for schools. It provides materials for schools and awards teachers for excellence in economic education.

Association for Humanistic Education (AHE)
P.O. Box 4054, University Sta.
Laramie, WY 82071-4054

The AHE is an international association that promotes humanistic thought through workshops, newsletters, and newspieces in and out of the schools.

Association for Humanistic Education
and Development (AHEAD)
c/o Amer. Assn. for Counseling and
Development.
5999 Stevenson Ave.
Alexandria, VA 22304

This association is a division of American Association for Counseling and Development and provides information on humanistic issues.

APPENDIX THREE

Organizational Resources

Citizens for Excellence in Education (CEE), P.O. Box 3200, Costa Mesa, CA 92628, (715) 546-5931

National Association of Christian Educators (NACE), P.O. Box 3200, Costa Mesa, CA 92628, (714) 546-5931

National Monitor of Education, Box 402, Alamo, CA 94507, (415) 945-6745

American Education Coalition, 721 2nd St. NE, Washington, D.C. 20002, (202) 546-0865

National Education Association (NEA), 1201 16th St. NW, Washington, DC 20036

Association of Christian Schools International (ACSI), P.O. Box 4097, Whittier, CA 90607, (213) 694-4791

Christian Home Educators Association (CHEA), P.O. Box 28644, Santa Ana, CA 92799-8644, (714) 537-5121

Creation Science Research Center, P.O. Box 23195, San Diego, CA 92123, (619) 569-8673

Institute for Creation Research, 10946 Woodside Ave. North, Santee, CA

Citizens for Educational Freedom, Rosslyn Plaza, Suite 805, 1611 N. Kent St., Arlington, VA 22209

Sex Respect Curriculum, Respect Inc., P.O. Box 349, Bradley, IL 60915-0349, (815) 939-0296

Teen-Aid (Sex Education Curriculum), N. 1330 Kalispell, Spokane, WA 99201

American Institute for Character Education, P.O. Box 12617, San Antonio, TX 78212-0617, (512) 734-5091

Bothered About Dungeons and Dragons, P.O. Box 5513, Richmond, VA 23220-5013

Educational Research Analysts, P.O. Box 7518, Longview, TX 75607-7518, (214) 753-5993

The National Council for Better Education, 1373 Van Dorn Street, Alexandria, Virginia 22304, (703) 684-4404

Catholics United for the Faith, 45 Union Ave., New Rochelle, NY 10801, (914) 235-9404

Teachers' Unions

National Education Association (NEA), 16th Street NW, Washington, DC 20036

National Council for Better Education, 1800 Diagonal Rd., Suite 240, Alexandria, VA 22314, (703) 739-2660

Concerned Educators Against Forced Unionism (CEAFU), 8001 Braddock, Rd, Springfield, VA 22314, (703) 321-8519

Blumenfeld Education Letter, P.O. Box 45161, Boise, ID 83711, (208) 322-4440

Free Congress Research and Education Foundation, 721 Second St. NE, Washington, DC 20002

Legal Information

Christian Legal Society, P.O. Box 1492, Merrifield, VA 22116, (703) 642-1070

The National Legal Foundation, P.O. Box 64845, Virginia Beach, VA 23464

Rutherford Institute, P.O. Box 7482, Charlottesville, VA 22906-7482, (804) 978-3888

The Christian Law Association, 100 Erieview Plaza, 34th Floor, Cleveland, OH 44114, (216) 696-3900

Western Center for Law and Religious Freedom, 1211 "H" Street, Suite A, Sacramento, CA 95814, (916) 447-411

The Catholic League for Religious and Civil Rights, 1100 West Wells Street, Milwaukee, WI 53233, (414) 289-0170

Political Organizations

American Coalition for Traditional Values, 12 C St. NW, Suite 850, Washington, DC 20001, (202) 628-2967

Christian Coalition, Box 1990, Chesapeake, VA 23327, (804) 424-2630

Biblical News Service, P.O. Box 10428, Costa Mesa, CA 92627, (714) 850-0349

Christian Action Council, 701 W. Broad St., Suite 405, Falls Church, VA 22046, (703) 237-2100

Christian Voice, P.O. Box 37002, Washington DC 20013, (202) 544-5202

Christian Voters League, Box 2995, Es-condido, CA 92025, (619) 743-3000

Coalition for Religious Freedom, 316 Pennsylvania Ave. SE, Suite 403, Washington DC 20003, (202) 544-5160

National Coalition of Concerned Christians, P.O. Box 756, Sprig, TX 77383

National Conservative Foundation, 618 S. Alfred St., Alexandria, VA 22314, (703) 548-0900

Traditional Values Coalition, 100 Anaheim Blvd., Suite 350, Anaheim, CA 92805, (714)520-0300

National Republican Party and National Democratic Party

Public Advocacy Groups

Concerned Women for America, 370 L'EnFant Promenade S.W., Suite 800, Washington, DC 20024, (202) 488-7000

Eagle Forum, Box 618, Alton, IL 60014, (314) 355-3080

Family Rights Coalition, P.O. Box 524, Crystal Lake, IL. 60014, (815) 455-2268

Focus on the Family, Colorado Springs, CO 80995-0001, (719) 531-5181

Heritage Foundation, 214 Massachusetts Ave. NE, Washington, DC 20002, (202) 546-4400

Point of View, 2290 Springlake, Ste 107, Dallas, TX 75234, 351-1212

National Federation for Decency. P.O. Drawer 2440, Tupelo, MS 38803, (601) 844-5036

Christian Action Council, 422 C St., NE., Washington, DC 20002

Accuracy in Media, 1275 K Street NW, Washington, DC 20005

Committee to Protect the Family, 8001 Forbes Place, Suite 102, Springfield, VA 22151

National Association of Evangelicals, 1023 15th Street NW, Suite 500, Washington, DC 20005, (202) 789-1011

The Roundtable, P.O. Box 11467, 3295 Poplar Ave., Memphis, TN 38111, (901) 458-3795

Chapter Four

1. Grady Lee, "Is the Future Safe For Our Children?" *Charasima and Christian Life* 16 (January 1991): 62

2. Washington (AP) Study, "Millions of Workers Struggle With Reading, Math, and Help Isn't On the Way" *Oshkosh Northwestern* (1992).

3. Philip Card, "Do You Believe in God?" Out of My Mind Columns, Sentinal Correspondent *Oshkosh Northwestern* (27 May 1992): 2E.

4. Joanne Jacobs, "Problem Isn't the Schools; It's the Systems," *Oshkosh Northwestern*, (9 August 1990).

5. *Humanist Manifestos, 1 & 2*, (Buffalo, NY, Prometheus Books, 1933, 1973), 8, 9, 16.

6. "Occult in the Classroom," *New Age Education Newsletter* (1990): 1.

7. Dr. Robert L. Simonds, "Floundering in the Educational Wasteland" *Free Enterprise Newsletter* 26 (1990): 4

8. John Eldredge, "Can NEA Change? Ask These Teachers," *Citizen* (17 September 1990).

9. Winnebago County, *Literacy Council 1990* Brochure (1990).

Chapter Five

1. Jon Schaffarzich and Gary Sykes, "NIE's Role in Curriculum Development: Finding, Policy Options, and Recommendations," (Washington, DC: National Institute of Education 8 February 1977), 3.

2. Galen J. Saylor, *"Who Planned the Curriculum"* (West Lafayette, IN: Kappa Delta Pi Press, 1982), 1.

3. Ibid., 11.

4. Ibid., 78.

5. Doug Zellmer, "Ghostbusters Invade the Grand" *Oshkosh Northwestern* (22 March 1992): 1.

6. "New Age Teaching May be in Your School System" Fundraising letter from *Concerned Women for America* Washington, DC.

7. "A policy report issued by Citizens for Excellence in Education" *New Age Education Newsletter* 5 (1990).

8. Mario D. Fantini, and Gerald Weistein, *Toward Humanistic Education–A Curriculum of Affect* (New York: Praeger Publishers, 1970), 218-219.

9. Ibid., 218-219.

10. Ibid., 219.

11. "Affective Education *Citizens for Excellence in Education* (1990).

12. "Brain Waves: Do You Know the Difference" *The Mel Gablers* (1991)

13. "Third-Grader Claims Psychological Injuries," *Education News Line* (October/November 1991).

14. David Llewellyn, *False Impressions: The 'Impressions' Reading Series Controversy*, (Sacramento, CA: Western Center for Law and Religious Freedom, 1990): 9.

15. Ibid., 9-10.

16. Ibid., 10.

17. Deborah Mendenhall, "Nightmarish Textbooks Await Your Kids," *Citizen* (17 September 1990): 4.

18. Ibid., 4.

19. "Quest Programs,"*The Mel Gablers*, Longview, TX (1988): 1.

20. Ibid., 1.

21. Janice and Gary Beebee, "Quest, Review & Analysis," Citizens for Excellence in Education,   (1987): 1.

22. "Questions and Answers on Quest," *Concerned Women for America*, (January 1991): 3.

23. "Tactics–A Program for Teaching Thinking, *The Mel Gablers*: 1-31.

24. "Educators Promote Politically Correct Curriculum," *Christian American* (May/June 1992): 14.

25. "Change, Adapt or Be Left Behind, Reformist Says," *News & Views*, (May 1992): 8.

26. Ibid., 4, 5.

27. Steve Aiken, *Dragon Slayer* (N.P.: N.D.), 3, 4.

28. Ibid., 4, 5.

29. *Scholastic Instructional Materials Catalogue* (Jefferson City, MO: Scholastic, Inc., 1992), 146.

30. *Avon Flare Camelot* (New York: Avon Books, 1991), 20, 33, 34, 42.

31. *Paperback Ave* (Charlotteville, NY: Education Paperbacks, 1991), 3, 16, 21, 25, 91.

32. *The Reading Writing Thinking Connection Pre-K to Adult* (Monroe, NY: Trillium Press), 2, 5, 7, 8, 9, 25.

Chapter Six

1. Dan Quayle, "The Family Values America Needs," *All About Issues* (September/October 1992): 22-24.

2. Howard Kirschenbaum and Simon B. Sidney, *Readings in Values Clarification* (Minneapolis, MN: Winston Press, Inc., 1973), 311-312.

3. Ibid., 312-313.

4. Education News Line, NACE/CEE (September/October 1990): 1.

5. Ibid., 1.

6. Jerrald R. Shive, *Social Studies as Controversy* (Pacific Palisades, CA: Goodyear Publishing Company, Inc., 1973), 55.

7. Ibid., 56.

8. Maury Smith, *Practical Guide to Value Clarification* (LaJolla, CA: University Associates, Inc., 1977): 20-21.

9. Ibid., 25-30.

10. Ibid., 31-35.

11. Ibid., 36-43.

12. Ibid., 44-49.

13. Ibid., 50-52.

14. Ibid., 53-57.

15. Ibid., 58-60.

16. Ibid., 61-63.

17. Ibid., 64-65.

18. Ibid., 66.

19. Ibid., 69.

20. Ibid., 71-73.

21. Ibid., 74-75.

22. Ibid., 112-113.

23. Ibid., 120.

24. Ibid., 121.

25. Ibid., 131-132.

26. Geri Curwin and Richard L. Curwin, *Learning Magazine, Developing Individual Values in the Classroom* (Palo Alto, CA: Learning Handbooks, 1974), 63-67.

27. Sidney B. Simon and Jay Clark, *Beginning Values Clarification Strategies For the Classroom* (San Diego, CA: Pennant Press, 1975), 121.

28. Ibid., 122.

29. Ibid., 132.

30. Ibid., 140.

31. Ibid., 144.

32. Ibid., 145-146.

33. Louis E. Roths, Merrill Harmin and Sidney B. Simon, *Values and Teaching Second Edition* (Columbus OH: Charles E. Merrill Publishing, 1976): 128-129.

34. Ibid., 128-129.

35. Ibid., 100.

36. Ibid., 137-139.

37. Louis E. Raths, Merril Harmin, Sidney B. Simon, *Values and Teaching Working with Values in the Classroom* (Columbus, OH: Merrill PublishingCo., 1966), 84.

38. Ibid., 84-85.

39. Ibid., 140-141.

40. Ibid., 247.

41. Ibid., 260-261.

42. Merril Harmin, Howard Kirschenbaum and Sidney B. Simon, *Clarifying Values Through Subject Matter. Applications for the Classroom* (Minneapolis, MN: Winston Press, Inc. 1973): 37-38.

43. Donald H. Peckenpaugh, *The School's Role as Moral Authority: "Moral Education" The Role of the School,* Association for Supervision and Curriculum Development (1977): 36.

44. Richard H. Hersh, Diana Pritchard Paolitto, Joseph Reimer, *Promoting Moral Growth* (New York, NY: Longman, Inc. 1979), 58-61.

45. John P. Dworetzky, Nancy J. Davis, *Human Development A Lifespan Approach* (St. Paul, MN: West Publishing Co., 1989), 236.

46. Dr. Roger Taylor, *Strengthening Your Program For*

Gifted Students (Bellevue, WA: Bureau of Education and Research, 1976), 146.

47. Ibid., 147.
48. Ibid., 148.
49. Ibid., 149.

Chapter Nine

1. *Focus,* (Madison, WI: Wisconson Association of School Board Policy, August 1986): 1,2.
2. People for Basic Education, Hand-out, Waukesha, WI (1987).
3. Ibid.

Chapter Ten

1. George E. Twente, II M.D., "The Damage of Mind Altering Techniques," *Education News Line,* (September/ October 1992): 5.

ORDER THESE HUNTINGTON HOUSE BOOKS !

_____	America Betrayed—Marlin Maddoux	$6.99 _____
_____	Angel Vision (A Novel)—Jim Carroll with Jay Gaines	5.99 _____
_____	*Battle Plan: Equipping the Church for the 90s—Chris Stanton	7.99 _____
_____	Blessings of Liberty—Charles C. Heath	8.99 _____
_____	Cover of Darkness (A Novel)—J. Carroll	7.99 _____
_____	Crystalline Connection (A Novel)—Bob Maddux	8.99 _____
_____	Deadly Deception: Freemasonry—Tom McKenney	7.99 _____
_____	The Delicate Balance—John Zajac	8.99 _____
_____	Dinosaurs and the Bible—Dave Unfred	12.99 _____
_____	*Don't Touch That Dial—Barbara Hattemer & Robert Showers	9.99/19.99 _____
_____	En Route to Global Occupation—Gary Kah	9.99 _____
_____	Exposing the AIDS Scandal—Dr. Paul Cameron	7.99 _____
_____	Face the Wind—Gloria Delaney	9.99 _____
_____	*False Security—Jerry Parks	9.99 _____
_____	From Rock to Rock—Eric Barger	8.99 _____
_____	Hidden Dangers of the Rainbow—Constance Cumbey	8.99 _____
_____	*Hitler and the New Age—Bob Rosio	9.99 _____
_____	The Image of the Ages—David Webber	7.99 _____
_____	Inside the New Age Nightmare—Randall Baer	8.99 _____
_____	*A Jewish Conservative Looks at Pagan America—Don Feder	9.99/19.99 _____
_____	*Journey Into Darkness—Stephen Arrington	9.99 _____
_____	Kinsey, Sex and Fraud—Dr. Judith A. Reisman & Edward Eichel (Hard cover)	19.99 _____
_____	Last Days Collection—Last Days Ministries	8.95 _____
_____	Legend of the Holy Lance (A Novel)—William T. Still	8.99/16.99 _____
_____	New World Order—William T. Still	8.99 _____
_____	*One Year to a College Degree—Lynette Long & Eileen Hershberger	9.99 _____
_____	*Political Correctness—David Thibodaux	9.99 _____
_____	Psychic Phenomena Unveiled—John Anderson	8.99 _____
_____	Seduction of the Innocent Revisited—John Fulce	8.99 _____
_____	"Soft Porn" Plays Hardball—Dr. Judith A. Reisman	8.99/16.99 _____
_____	*Subtle Serpent—Darylann Whitemarsh & Bill Reisman	9.99 _____
_____	Teens and Devil-Worship—Charles G.B. Evans	8.99 _____
_____	To Grow By Storybook Readers—Janet Friend	44.95 per set _____
_____	Touching the Face of God—Bob Russell (Paper/Hardcover)	8.99/18.99 _____
_____	Twisted Cross—Joseph Carr	9.99 _____
_____	*When the Wicked Seize a City—Chuck & Donna McIlhenny with Frank York	9.99 _____
_____	Who Will Rule the Future?—Paul McGuire	8.99 _____
_____	*You Hit Like a Girl—Elsa Houtz & William J. Ferkile	9.99 _____

* _New Title_   Shipping and Handling   _____
                                           Total   _____

AVAILABLE AT BOOKSTORES EVERYWHERE or order direct from:
Huntington House Publishers • P.O. Box 53788 • Lafayette, LA 70505
Send check/money order. For faster service use VISA/MASTERCARD
call toll-free 1-800-749-4009.

Add: Freight and handling, $3.50 for the first book ordered, and $.50 for each additional book up to 5 books.

Enclosed is $——————— including postage.
VISA/MASTERCARD#_____ Exp. Date ————
Name _____
Address _____
City, State, Zip code_____